Journey Th

by

Anthony F. Raimondo. PhD

First Edition - Titled - Journey Through Revelation
Copy Rights July, 18, 2017
Case # 1-5638408281
Anthony Raimondo, PhD
All Rights Reserved
ISBN: 9781973298298

No part of this publication may be reproduced in a stored system or transmitted in any form, electronic, mechanical, photocopying, recording, or otherwise, without the written permission of the author.

Website: acceleratingevolutionllc.net
docspeaksshow@gmail.com
https://www.youtube.com/c/drraimondo
Clifton, NJ USA 07012

Acknowledgment

I was in my office/studio, researching a topic for my YouTube show, when the LORD spoke to me and said, "I want you to write." Then, an angel spoke and said, "I will guide you as to what to write." I was then inspired to write this commentary on the Book of Revelation. I did receive insights as I researched, prayed, and meditated about specific symbols. It took a great deal of time and prayer to complete this book. In the Book of Revelation, you will notice that the Lord Jesus Christ and angels provide the Apostle John with what to write.

I want to give thanks and praise to the Lord God and His Holy Spirit through Jesus Christ for giving me the inspiration and ideas for this commentary, for without Their guidance, I would not have been able to write it.

Next, I wish to thank my family and friends for letting me bend their ears with my thoughts and for Patty Sadallah and Larry Silver, two extraordinary individuals who prayed weekly for successful completion. I also wish to thank my wife, Fedela, and sons, Antony and Jared, for their support. A very special thank you to Gerald Del Colle for the marvelous spiritual horse painting he provided for this book's cover.

Finally, thank you, the reader, for reading this book. I hope you gain the blessing that the book of Revelation provides and that the information also helps you discern much of the false teaching concerning humanity's future.

Anthony "Doc" Raimondo, Ph.D. & Th.D.

Preamble

I was sitting in my small studio to produce my radio/video show, Doc Speaks Show, a video version on YouTube, while I was meditating and praying about a topic for my Christian-based show. The Lord spoke, and I saw his faint image dressed in white. He said, "I want you to write." I saw another faint image of another being also dressed in white, and he said, "I am here to help." After that, the images vanished. Ideas for the writing began to come quickly. The concepts drew me to the Book of Revelation and to an intense probing to write. I felt the need to write this paragraph after writing about half of the chapters in Revelation. The Still Small Voice of the Holy Spirit would give me a clue, a word that would provide the answer I needed to continue writing. Often, a word would be accompanied by an image so that the meaning would be exact. It would spark the response I was thinking. I read, researched, and meditated on one chapter at a time and did not move to the next until it was clear I had addressed it appropriately.

One must keep in mind the Blessing and Curse attached to John's writing content when writing on the substance or the meaning of the symbolism in the

Canon Book of Revelation. Which is the adding or the subtracting of the material presented? It would include all misinterpretations of the symbols used. Therefore one takes a significant risk in even translating John's original manuscript. In doing so, one could be adding or subtracting from it. Individuals, including myself, are at high risk of being lost forever in the Lake of Fire for misrepresenting the book's content. By misinterpreting the material, you have added or subtracted it from the original. Also, translation errors create an additional problem. We also need to keep in mind that Satan only added a single word and changed the whole meaning of a sentence; the serpent added: "not" "You shall not surely die." (Genesis 3:4)

There are several schools of thought on the material. All may have missed the point and are, therefore, cursed. It is a simple observation because another subtracted what one group may add. These are the various camps: Premillennialism, Postmillennialism, Amillennialism, and Idealism. One theologian did not even wish to consider a Historical perception. I will not take the time and space to provide in-depth differences, dealing with the thousand years mentioned at the end of Revelation and the return of Christ. However, just on the prefix of pre and post, one or both need to be corrected. The others are buffet styles, some of this or that, and the possibility of leaving something out.

Finally, a camp called Historical attempts to put things in a historical, chronological pattern. There are also four different ways of interrupting Revelation once again; we have the problem of false teaching and the risk of the curse attached to Revelation. There are four primary ways of approaching the Book of Revelation. First, the futurist view puts all the events before Christ's return. Second, the preterits see Revelation as past events before the Temple's destruction in 70 AD and the dissolution of the Roman Empire in the fifth century. This notion is wrong for two simple reasons: the Roman Empire's second capital was in Turkey, which survived until the 15th century. Second, the other problem is Christ has yet to return. Third, the historicist interprets Revelation as representing chronological historical events in sequential order. Lastly, the idealist views the visions in Revelation as symbolically describing the period.

There is another critical point to consider. Much of the theology written about the Book of Revelation is based incorrectly because the interruption is before the restoration of Israel's nation. These same individuals also neglect that Israel is no longer a nation at the time of the writing by at least 20 to 25 years. Therefore, suggesting that Rome is the nation that was and is again through the Roman Catholic Church is nonsense. We now have Israel, a country that was, is not, and is again. Rome was not a past nation during the writing but was still in power. One can say that Christianity is the religion of the USA, but it is not the government. Israel is different in that the nation is in a relationship with God. Therefore, the faith of Judaism is part of the state, based on the covenants God has made with her. One would hope that a nation would honor and respect God, but in many cases, they do not. The Roman Empire making Christianity its national religion and abandoning paganism did not make the church a government or a nation; it merely made it the acceptable worship of the land. Also, the church is a collection of many countries. Therefore, the relationship between God, Christ, and the church differs significantly.

When we view the Book of Revelation as the story's conclusion, we understand the closing events more accurately. The Bible is a single story about a relationship between God and a particular nation. From a literary standpoint, the Bible is a saga like the Game of Thrones. It is a story of a nation of people over a long period. The Book of Revelation is the final book of the saga with both a tragic and joyful ending.

The opening "Chapter is Genesis," which is the prologue. The definition of the title is the generations. It leads to the nation of Israel as the protagonist of the canon. Israel, introduced in Exodus, and Israel is a significant character in the saga and is portrayed as a female from this point on. Her role is the collective consciousness of the people of Israel. She reflects the collective attitudes, morals, and emotions of the leaders who influence the people. They are much like their ancient mother, Eve, who was tempted by the illusion of something better. This illusion is of the world domination of a Messiah; a world-ruling king is also the reason for the rejection of Jesus Christ. The ordinary people reflect Adam, who mindlessly accepts the forbidden fruit from Eve after remaining passive and not stopping her from being tempted. In the opening act of the Drama, we have a wife who betrays her husband by being seduced by the serpent. Throughout the Drama, Israel and Judah, time and time again, turn from God and listen to the serpent.

In the saga, the protagonist, Israel, is assisted, guided, and ruled by individual characters that become her voice of moral reason provided by God. Though not perfect, individuals have been found worthy through their faith and obedience to God. God has placed the twelve tribes in Egypt, where she prospers by Joseph's cunning abilities for a time. He enslaves the Egyptians while enriching his brothers and their families until a new pharaoh puts them as a nation into slavery for a period of four hundred years.

The ordeal kept the twelve tribes together to form one nation, Israel. It was also a means of keeping them united and, finally, creating a bond, a relationship between God and this new nation. So it is the story's beginning with God and Israel, between God and His "Bride." Through Moses, God gives His "Bride" the law that she must follow to stay in good standing with Him, but as in the prologue, conflict continues to surface due to the antagonist's constant temptation and the people's stubbornness.

Israel is God's protagonist to be His model and representative as a light for the other nations. She is to be a light for the world so that all humankind can fully fellowship with God. However, throughout the Drama, Israel fails; she becomes two sisters, one worse than the other, a divided house between Israel and Judah. The drama continues through a series of episodes until the final event, where God can no longer hold back from punishing Israel and all other nations. She fails both in her righteousness and has a light for other countries.

In this drama, there is one primary antagonist between God and His Bribe, Satan, the chief nemesis. He first appears in Genesis, the prologue. He is the voice of evil that first emerges in the serpent who tempts Eve. Samael, aka Lucifer, a Cherubim, has gone evil and is called Satan in Job. In Revelation, Samael's Hebrew meaning is "venom of God"; he is the Dragon. Throughout the drama, he causes separation between God and man and between God and Israel. His chief desire and purpose are to destroy man and to take the position on God's Throne. He causes a rebellion in Heaven with a third of the angels taking his side, for he accuses God of Tyranny. Many of Satan's earthly followers preach this very same view. The battle he creates on earth is by deception too corrupt and to the final destruction of man. The antagonist also has deceived individuals who perform his work in the physical world.

God, the Author of the Drama, is also a significant character in His Saga. God is the principal character in the drama, constantly dealing with an adulteress wife, Israel. He punishes and forgives her, but no sooner is she forgiven than she is back to being the Harlot.

The story's opening scene takes place inside the Garden of Eden, where Lucifer, through the serpent, first seduces Eve to rebel, then tempts and betrays her husband against God through disobedience, as she had done.

Throughout the drama, the land west and north of the Tigris and Euphrates Rivers is where the action occurs. It is the setting for the theater. Keep in mind that the author of this drama is also the director, and like any fair play, it has only one primary location. It is a flaw of many theologians who need knowledge of fundamental literary elements and presume settings without examining the author's descriptions.

The secondary Gentile characters are often instruments of God used to punish and correct Israel's nation, keeping in mind that the principal protagonist of the account is always the nation of Israel. All clues and symbolism point to her and her offspring. Throughout Biblical history, the progeny of Israel's tribes are the players shaping and moving the events through the plot of each of the significant acts of the forty-seven books, with an additional nineteen letters addressing the new covenant for both Jew and Gentile alike. However, the key players in and behind the scenes are always those of the tribes of Israel.

During the final scenes, before the curtain closes, a small number of Israelite offspring have repented and have accepted the one and only true Messiah. The Son sacrificed His own life to reconcile the progeny of Israel and other nations to God. It resembles a Greek Tragedy, for many of Israel's offspring are lost, and therefore, Israel never overcomes her sinful nature. As a result, Israel never achieves victory over the antagonist. Israel reaches the greatness that she has longed for, but in doing so, Israel fails to be the Bribe God desires. Throughout the saga, Israel/Judea illustrates being the unfaithful wife, with the Levite tribe of priests creating their form of belief rather than accepting their Messiah, the Talmud inspired by Satan through the voice of humanity. Like her mother, Eve, she has done so many times before; she listens to the sound of the serpent.

Having prepared a very brief overview of the Bible, we can now examine the final act of this drama, the account's conclusion, as if the curtain has already closed. We will stand with John in Heaven, recalling the events as they took place, one after the other. With the help of Jesus Christ, I intend, through the Holy Spirit's guidance, to guide the reader through the Book of Revelation. We will examine it from two points of view as John perceived the events in his future and as we perceive the occurrences from the position that some are in our past, some may be taking place, while others have yet to occur. I intend for the reader to look at Revelation without any particular doctrine. We shall let the matter speak for itself to obtain the true meaning of God's vision of John. We have a script, the stage in place, and the action is taking place; we, the audience, observe and witness the drama unfold.

As we journey through Revelation, we need to understand the meaning of the symbols. It can quickly lead a person astray when viewed by a particular religious doctrine. It is the largest area of misinterpretation. When we approach the material in this manner, our bias blinds us. We must also remember that the final episode of the Biblical Drama, Revelation, is an Interactive theatre piece, where the fourth wall of the stage is down, and the reader is now a part of the drama should anything be added or deleted.

The desire to make the symbols fit a particular group or outcome contaminates the Master's Words. One cannot dilute or degrade the Author, God's very Words and Images. It often occurs by scanning the Bible to find a single verse that could fit the symbol but could miss the mark entirely. It is often the case with the so-called Anti-Christ, False Prophet, and the Harlot, giving them a false motive, a mistaken identity, and appearance. Much of this misleading interpretation has its roots in the antagonist to create further conflict. The audience in this interactive production is either for or against the antagonist. Before all else, one needs to keep in mind the whole storyline of the saga and its main characters.

When we examine most of the material, the emphasis is always on the Roman Empire, the Church of Rome, or an individual of Rome, but this is not a correct interpretation. Several clues would suggest that these are incorrect. The first view should always apply the evidence and symbols to the account's main protagonist. It is essential because God's entire narrative deals with His relationship with the people of the Tribes of Israel and then the Gentiles.

The clues and symbols help us, the audience, identify the flaws in the main character or provide insight into the antagonist's characteristics. The minor players in God's narrative are the individuals who represent and support the major players. When examining the symbols and clues in God's description, we, the reader, must be careful in identifying correctly the who, what, where, when, why, and how of the Lord's manuscript. Therefore, another critical factor in understanding the events is the setting.

Where this action takes place is also crucial in discerning the players and their motives. In a homicide, the detective is always interested in the crime scene. Well, we need to apply the same forensics to study Revelation. We know that Satan is Israel's number one nemesis because she is the love of God. God has blessed her above all other nations. Therefore, who would be Satan's primary target but Israel? Israel had a daughter, and she is Christian, and Satan hates her more than he hates her mother.

As we read through the Book of Revelation, it will become evident that the area of concern, the scene for the drama and the crime scene, is in the Mesopotamian Valley, the cradle of civilization. It was the location of the Garden of Eden; it was where Adam and Eve committed the first sin; it was where the serpent told the first lie; it was where Cain committed the first murder; and it was the sight of the early graves. It was where Nimrod tried to build the tower of Babel, where Nebuchadnezzar made the Golden Kingdom, and where he had a dream concerning the future of his kingdom. It is where Satan has his throne, Abaddon is held captive, four angels are locked up in the Euphrates River, and the synagogue of Satan stands. It is the location where three cities stand on seven hills. There is no need to go to another theatre or seek another crime scene when the action occurs here, in Babylon's territory, south of Havilah.

John, Christ's secretary, writes to seven communities called churches that will receive the manuscript of the final act of God's Narrative Drama. These seven communities are the first group to perform in this last act of God's Drama. Their roles receive a critique, actors notes from Christ the Director on their performance thus far, those done well and those areas that require improvement, and a warning of termination, if there are no improvements. These are characteristics that Christ needs improvement from these seven churches during the first century, and he warns them that Satan is nearby and in their midst. Of course, these same critiques are for other churches experiencing the same attack and corruption from Satan. However, these seven letters can provide insight for future churches with all of God's Words.

John is taking dictation; however, he has not been given a single word to the believers in Rome and many other churches with Jewish and Gentile believers in Him. He is taking dictation and recording the images he has seen. These events are after the deaths of Peter and Paul. They both worked to establish a church in Rome. Jesus Christ did not order John to write to the church outside of ancient Babylon's territory, only to seven churches in Asia Minor, today's Turkey, and not anywhere in Italy. It is the Northern portion of Nebuchadnezzar's kingdom. The drama is to end on the stage where it began.

Another theatrical error in establishing a setting for the final act's events is the location of the capital of Rome. Most of the written material continuously overlooks one fundamental fact: the Roman Empire had two capitals, not one. This one point missing alone can destroy the entire credibility of the interpretation.

Daniel chapter 2 verse 33 states, 'its legs of iron, its feet partly of iron and partly of baked clay.' The word, legs is plural, meaning more than one. Also, it states feet, not foot. A human body has a right and left leg, with a right and left foot. Rome had a capital in the West, Rome, and a capital in the East, Constantinople, today's city of Istanbul, with each city built like Jerusalem on seven hills.

If we are looking at a statue in Nebuchadnezzar's dream face to face, the figure's right leg would be to our left, just as viewing a map, Rome would be to our left, the West. Istanbul, the second capital to the East, is our right, but it would be to the left of Rome. The left side in Roman times was called 'sinistram' in English sinister. A word that means or denotes evil. There, we have a clue that one setting is more evil than another. With this one change in the location, we have a different possible meaning for Revelation's symbols. A theologian set designer would argue that Rome is sitting on seven hills. They fail to say or understand that Istanbul, Mecca, Jerusalem, and ancient Babylon are all built on seven hills and at least 14 other major cities, including New York City, with an idol on the Hudson River.

Since Istanbul is the other Roman Capital built on seven hills, we need to examine scenes from Turkey because this was the northern portion of Nebuchadnezzar's Kingdom. One should always keep in mind that the western border of the Kingdom of Babylon is Israel. In Daniel 2:29, "As Your Majesty was lying there, your mind turned to things to come, and the revealer of mysteries showed you what is going to happen." Daniel explains that the King was concerned about the future of his Kingdom, the reason for the dream. His Kingdom is represented by a single statue that goes bad from the head down until it is no more due to idol worship, sexual immorality, and sorcery.

The Eastern Roman capital fell to the Islamic Ottoman Turks in 1453. It gives Nebuchadnezzar's dream one more consideration. Another vital point to examine is that the feet were all made of clay. It is a right and a left foot, each representing Islam. The two revile factions, the Sunni and the Sufism, each within five nations. Again, the scene of the crime points to where it all began. Also, the statue in the dream can only represent the territory of Babylon—the only correct setting for God's Drama.

In this presentation, we shall review an alternative approach to the possible conclusion to the final act in God's Narrative, the Revelation events. You will notice that I will be using the New International Version. Also, chapter markings with a number in parentheses, while the verse will begin with a number. We will start our journey with Chapter 12 as the prelude to the final act since Chapter 12 sets the stage as a brief narrative summary of the events leading up to God's Drama's last act. I will also use a more literary approach to our investigation and view the event with John as part of the audience.

The letters to the seven churches can be separated from the book and sent individually to each church. They are a warning, announcement, and instructions for improving righteousness with Christ's teachings' continued practice. It is interesting to note that the recipient of the letters is an angel of the church. The Book of Revelation's remaining chapters represent the 'Great Tribulation's total visions,' the final act of God's Drama. The 'Great Tribulation' final scene concludes with Daniel's seven-year period. Still, it is the total duration referred to as the Gentiles' time, a period between the ascension and return of Jesus Christ.

It will be apparent to the reader that Chapter 12 cannot occur in the future since the events of the chapter are a symbolic, literal summary of critical events of John's Gospel. It illustrates the Dragon's efforts to devour the offspring that would crush its head. (Genesis 3:15) Without Christ's sacrifice, the book of Revelation has no purpose. Therefore it is clear that chapter 12 had to take place before a worthy Christ could open the Seven Seals.

Introduction

The Book of Revelation is God's final chapter dealing with Adam and Eve's offspring, Noah's sons and their wives, and the nemesis Satan the Dragon. It is also called the Revelation to John, the Apocalypse of John, or just Revelation or Apocalypse. Its title originates from the first word of the text, written in Koine Greek: apokalypsis, meaning "unveiling" or "revelation." The Book of Revelation is the only apocalyptic document in the New Testament canon; it also occupies a central place in Christian eschatology.

The secretary names himself in the introduction as "John"; however, there are those who dispute his identity. The agreed date for Revelation's writing is around 95AD, with John the Apostle dying around 100AD, at the end of the first century. Second-century Christian writers such as Justin Martyr, Irenaeus, Clement of Alexandria, and Melito, the bishop of Sardis, may have had a copy of the original and verbal account identify John the Apostle as the "John" of Revelation.

Modern skeptic scholars believe that nothing can identify the author except that he was a Christian prophet. These are the false teachers who characterize the author as a putative figure they call "John of Patmos." Those who distort God's Word support the nemesis of God and humanity. This view would treat the work as total fiction, which is precisely what the antagonist desires. Traditional sources date the book to emperor Domitian's reign (AD 81-96), providing more evidence of John the Apostle as the author since these dates are within his lifetime.

The book contains three literary genres: the epistolary, the apocalyptic, and the prophetic, both literal and symbolic forms. It begins with John on the island of Patmos in the Aegean, off Turkey's coast and not far from the Seven Churches. First, he addresses a letter to the "Seven Churches of Asia." Next, John describes Heaven and the Throne of God's image and a series of prophetic visions dealing with punishment. It includes these figures, Angels, a Dragon, the Whore of Babylon and the Beast of the Sea, and one of the Earth. Finally, the book climaxes with the Second Coming of Jesus and a New Heaven and New Earth.

I chose to add some verses from the Book of Enoch because they clarify the Book of Revelation elements. Interestingly, the same second-century notable Christians believed it to be a sacred book; Irenaeus and Clement of Alexandria each stated the Book of Enoch as sacred. Irenaeus continues by assigning to the Book of Enoch an authenticity analogous to that of Mosaic literature. It affirms that Enoch, a man, filled the office of God's messenger to the angels.

Tertullian flourished at the end of the first and beginning of the second century, the period at the writing and death of John the Apostle, the author of Revelation. He admitted that some do not receive the "Scripture of Enoch " because of being excluded from the Hebrew Canon. He speaks of the author as "the most ancient prophet, Enoch," and that the book is a divinely inspired autograph of that immortal patriarch, preserved by Noah in the ark or miraculously reproduced through the inspiration of the Holy Spirit. Tertullian adds, "But as Enoch has spoken in the same scripture of the Lord, and every Scripture suitable for edification is divinely inspired," therefore, let us reject nothing that glorifies God the Father and His Son Jesus Christ.

It is likely the Jewish leaders disavowed the book of Enoch as they had done with many of the books of the prophets because it speaks of Christ. It is not surprising since they did not receive him when He talked to them. In itself is evidence of the character these leaders portray. They play the role of minor antagonists, the lesser villains, who secretly cause the inevitable downfall of members of their synagogue for the sole purpose of maintaining wealth and control. In God's Saga of 66 books, what character, person, or group has knowingly rejected scripture to hide the identity of the Son of God? The answer was the Jewish leaders of Christ's day who desired a Messiah for world domination.

When one reads the Book of Enoch, one can notice verses that appear in the New Testament, even statements made by Christ, such as, "It would be far better for that man if he had never been born!" (Matt 26:24) Jude and Paul have also made similar statements in their letters. In Jude 1:14, it is written, "Enoch also, the seventh from Adam, prophesied of these, saying, 'Behold, the Lord cometh with ten thousands of his saints, to execute judgment upon all, and to convict all that are ungodly among them of all their ungodly deeds, which they have ungodly committed, and of all their hard speeches which ungodly sinners have spoken against Him.'" Here, Jude is quoting Enoch. Also, the image is similar to what John witnesses here in Revelation Chapter Fourteen.

Paul also quotes Enoch in Titus 1:12 "A prophet from their people said of them 'Cretans are always liars, wicked brutes, lazy gluttons.'" There are some other examples to present. However, that would become a series of pages in itself. The purpose of introducing Enoch in this material is to offer some additional insight into the events in the Book of Revelation. Like Revelation, the Book of Enoch is a book of prophecy of the coming flood, but also a glance at the final scene in God's last act of end-time judgment before His destruction of the present world, creating a new world free of evil.

I wish to point out one more overlooked concept of the Book of Revelation. As in well-written essays and non-fiction literary manuscripts, the end reflects the beginning. God, the author of this manuscript, uses the device of drawing back to Genesis for seven periods or days. The Book of Revelation suggests seven periods: one of darkness, to Noah, to Moses the Law, three Savior Jesus, followed by the periods of the Seals, the Trumpet and the Bowels, and finally, the day of rest, a period of peace the Millennium, ending with a New Day, a New World. The Book of Revelation comes full circle with the completion of God's plan. Today is the period of Trumpets.

Prologue, Greetings, and Doxology

The text begins with a similar format that Paul uses in his letters. The style would be typical of the day. However, in the opening, it is addressed to the Seven Churches of the Lord Christ. John is writing as a secretary and also points to Christ's return Rev. 1:7: "Look, He is coming with the clouds, and every eye will see Him, even those who pierced Him; and all peoples on earth will mourn because of Him. So shall it be! Amen!"

The text begins with a similar format that Paul uses in his letters. In his opening, John believes that the audience he is writing will witness the following events. He thinks that it will all take place in his present generation. "Truly I tell you, this generation will certainly not pass away until all these things have happened." (Matt 24:34 NIV) Based on that statement, even Christ believed that events would begin to happen soon, and they do. The fact that Jesus Christ is warning these seven church communities is an indication that activities are underway. These are not symbolic churches of some future time, as some may suggest, but churches at the very time of receiving the letters.

In the first scene, John confers to the reader that he is but a servant with orders to write. The substance of the information is directly from the Lord. He presents this to assure the audience that the data is not of his imagination but what Christ has revealed to him. To add credibility to the message, he includes his Identity and the writing time's present location. Members of the various communities would have learned that John the Beloved Apostle is in exile on the Island of Patmos for the audience to receive the message as genuine. These details and a messenger would be needed to convince the audience of its authentic message. Today, we can send a message via the internet with our picture or even a video file, which clarifies they we are the messenger.

John's purpose is to ensure the information is accurate. John would have known of false teaching and the slander circulating during the past 50 years or more before his exile. John would also be aware of the early Christian Church's enemies to discredit any message of the Lord Jesus Christ. Therefore, the source of the material needed to link to Christ through one of his credulous followers directly. This inscription added to the opening was traditionally part of the beginning of a letter. The letters of Paul demonstrate this direct link to Jesus. The messages would have been delivered by a courier who would have orally verified the author of the sealed manuscript and from where it came; this would prove that the material was authentic. Also, the seal would ascertain that the letter is in its original form. Finally, a respected elder of the community would receive the letter. The elder would then share the content with the community.

Having established the opening and John's credibility, let's jump forward to Chapter 12 of Revelation, a symbolic, metaphoric summary of the whole saga before this final episode. One more detail is that writers in this period did not often write in chronological order to emphasize a point. David Limbaugh, in his book "The True Jesus," underscores this very point.

The Dragon and the Dragon Slayer

John now sees a vision of a Woman and the Dragon

Since the ancient writers did not often use chronological order in much of their writing, we can see that the material in Chapter 12 is a prelude to the events that precede everything that John witnesses and records. The inspiration was to start this commentary here. You will notice that the events that John witnessed in this chapter are in his past. The first act of a drama introduces the major characters and the conflict within the narrative. The nemesis of Man, Lucifer, who desires to destroy man and God's creation, uses the serpent to perform the deed — having succeeded in man's downfall, both Lucifer and the serpent share the same fate as a result of God's curse. Thus, from that moment, Lucifer seeks to destroy the offspring of Eve. "And I will put enmity between you and the woman and between your seed and her seed; He shall bruise you on the head, And you shall bruise him on the heel." (Genesis 3:5 NIV) From this moment, the saga of Good vs Evil begins with a villain doomed for all eternity. Being cursed only inflames Satan's anger.

The setting now changes; man is cast out of the Garden and travels eastward. "After he drove the man out, he placed on the East side of the Garden of Eden cherubim with a flaming sword flashing back and forth to guard the way to the tree of life" (Genesis 3:24 NIV). Adam and Eve enter into a land that one day will become Babylon. The site of God's drama where He will destroy darkness and create the future world of light. The Saga began in Genesis 1 states, "In the beginning, God created the heavens and the earth. 2 Now the earth was formless and empty, darkness was over the surface of the deep, and the Spirit of God was hovering over the waters." (NIV) We shall see in the concluding chapter of Revelation the completion of God's plan. The destruction of darkness and all that it embraces, to a New Heaven and Earth of only His Glorious Light, light must shine forth from it to destroy darkness and all of its evil and death.

The dragon now takes center stage and begins by having righteous Abel killed to prevent righteous offspring. The serpent assumes he can avoid the curse that is upon his head by inflaming Cain's jealousy. (Genesis: 4) In time, Eve's progeny would be a father of 12 tribes, and from the tribe of Judah, there would come a virgin from the House of David, who would give birth to the dragon slayer. The dragon knows of God's plan and is determined to prevent it.

Let's examine our clue cards to clarify the characters in God's Drama to clarify the definition of the word dragon. The word dragon first appears in English from the Old French dragon in the early 13th century. It came from the Latin draconem (nominative draco), meaning "huge serpent," from the Greek word δράκων, drakon (genitive drakontos, δράκοντος) "serpent, giant sea-fish." The Greek and Latin terms both referred to any great serpent. It would also apply to the serpent of Genesis, only symbolically more massive to emphasize Satan's degree of evilness; this image has created a false picture of Satan's beauty that he uses for deception. A terrifying figure with horns, scaly red skin, and a tail would frighten someone away. Lucifer is, however, a cherub and angel of beauty who can lure you into temptation.

The Dragon would continue to provoke evil from his place in Heaven. (Job) Lucifer the Dragon must have rejoiced at the time of the flood to see humankind destroyed, thinking the offspring could not 'crush his head,' but soon, he would realize his need to start a new one. Once again, he begins his work on Noah's children. Ham, having laughed at his father's nakedness, his son, is cursed to be a servant to his brothers. (Gen.9:20–27) It will cause division that will lead to war and killing. The Dragon tries to prevent a virgin from the tribe of Judah from David's house. For Serpent knows she will become a mother of many through her offspring destined to crush the Dragon's head under his foot. The long-awaited dragon slayer arrives, and the Dragon is ready to destroy him.

John envisions what he writes in chapter 12: "A great sign appeared in heaven: a woman clothed with the sun, with the moon under her feet, and on her head a crown of twelve stars." Here, the Supreme Author places Mary in a custom of virgin purity that shines as bright as the sun; at her feet, the Supreme Director sets a footstool for she is above other women and a crown on her head. The diadem symbolizes that she is queen over the 12 tribes of Israel and those who worship her son, who is King. The sun also represents power, for she now has power, and the moon is a symbol of time and space since it is her footstool; she has victory over both time and space through her son Jesus. Some theologians wish to make this a sign in the night sky in the constellation of Virgo, but the following verse would illustrate this as incorrect.

2 "She was pregnant and was crying out in birth pains and the agony of giving birth. 3 And another sign appeared in heaven: behold, a great red dragon, with seven heads and ten horns, and on his heads seven diadems." Again, the Supreme Director places the ultimate villain in custom to symbolize the character of man's nemesis. We see the actor on stage as a giant red, scaly snake to demonstrate the anger and hatred this slime creature has for man. Our villain appears with seven heads, each one to represent the seven deadly sins. The horns illustrate the ultimate depth of his sinful nature and the diadems, for he rules over these vices. Keep in mind this image is not of his appearance but his evil character.

4 "His tail swept down a third of the stars of heaven and cast them to the earth. And the dragon stood before the woman who was about to give birth so that when she bore her child, he might devour it. 5 She gave birth to a male child, one who is to rule over all the nations with a rod of iron, but her child was caught up to God and his throne, 6 and the woman fled into the wilderness, where she has a place prepared by God, in which she is to receive nourishment for 1,260 days." Here is an added side note: you may never hear of the birth of Jesus Christ. Isaiah prophecies

this, "Before she goes into labor, she gives birth; before the pains come upon her, she delivers a son. Who has heard of such as this? Who has seen such things?" (Isaiah 66:7-8 NIV) Joseph, her husband, witnessed it. It may not be in the Gospel, but it was to be a sign that this is indeed the birth of the Messiah. 2 "She was pregnant and was crying out in birth pains and the agony of giving birth. 3 And another sign appeared in heaven: behold, a great red dragon, with seven heads and ten horns, and on his heads seven diadems." I shall repeat, again, the Supreme Director places the ultimate villain in custom to symbolize the character of man's nemesis as a giant red, scaly snake to demonstrate the anger and hatred this slime creature has for man. Humanities villain appears with seven heads, each one to represent the seven deadly sins. With horns to illustrate the ultimate depth of his sinful nature and the diadems, for he rules over these vices. Again, this image is not his appearance but his evil character, yet Satan is a beautiful cherub in appearance.

Cue card notes:

Here is a series of brief scenes: first, the dragon is ready for the kill, Mary gives a painless birth, the ascension of Jesus Christ, the final picture in the series is Christ on his throne, and finally, Mary must go into hiding.

Satan Thrown Down to Earth

7 "Now war arose in Heaven, Michael and his angels fighting against the dragon. And the dragon and his angels fought back, 8 but he was defeated, and there

was no longer any place for them in heaven. 9 And the great dragon was thrown down, that ancient serpent, who is called the devil and Satan, the deceiver of the whole world—he was thrown down to the earth, and his angels were thrown down with him. 10 And I heard a loud voice in heaven, saying, 'Now the salvation and the power and the kingdom of our God and the authority of his Christ have come, for the accuser of our brothers is thrown down, who accuses them day and night before our God. 11 And they have conquered him by the blood of the Lamb and by the word of their testimony, for they loved not their lives even unto death. 12 Therefore, rejoice, O heavens, and you who dwell in them! But woe to you, O earth and sea, for the devil has come down to you in great wrath because he knows that his time is short!'"

The Author/God submits a poetic symbol of removing Lucifer and a third of the angels from the original station in Heaven to Earth, using his tail, meaning by the foul excrement of his accusations and through vile pleasures of evil. He persuaded a third of the angels using his fowl deception to do his bidding. As the drama unfolds, we witness that even angels experience this supervillain's temptation to do evil. "The sons of God saw that the daughters of humans were beautiful, and they married any of them they chose." (Genesis 6:2 NIV) The Book of Enoch presents this episode in greater detail. However, God is providing us with evidence of the degree of Lucifer's evil nature.

From these few verses, it is clear that we have a brief history of the birth of Jesus Christ and the escape into Egypt. He had caused Herod's heart to be jealous and fearful of losing his throne. As a result, he had boy offspring in Bethlehem up to the age of two killed. It must have pleased the dragon in thinking the deed of successfully killing boy children also murdered Jesus. The madness continues today. In America, States and the Federal Congress are making abortion legal even after birth. Satan desires to kill Christ's followers before they are born.

Clue card review:

We know from Matthew 2:13 that the woman exits the scene and, for a time, with the child and her faithful husband, protector, hides from the dragon in Egypt. Here, the Author leaves out any narrative of faithful Joseph, but the action illustrates that Joseph is the man Adam should have been. The story continues, and the party of three returns to Israel because Herod the Great's son kills him. Here, the Supreme/Author/Director provides the audience with a window into His judgment method where the punishment fits the crime. The Jackal, as a result of fear, jealousy, and greed, is motivated by the villain to kill God's Son. Herod's last appearance on the stage is experiencing God's retribution law known to all as Karma, so we read his son kills him. Three decades later, the grand villain performs God's patiently awaited moment when the serpent attacks the heel of the offspring of Eve, and in doing so, her offspring will crush his head. The Supreme Author has created the ultimate example of the antonym for the tragic hero, the supervillain who destroys himself.

Let's flashback to before the villain successfully kills his enemy, the Lamb of God. The Jackal had failed more than three decades before. Now, he decides to use Harlot's help to stir the people against the Lamb of God since her seduction methods may be more efficient. Now, the serpent knew that the Harlot, religious leaders, would quickly seek the Son of God's death once He made a claim. However, God had planned it by creating the penalty for blasphemy during the time of Moses. (Leviticus 24:10-23 NIV) God's plan out of love was to sacrifice Himself for the punishment of sin. Therefore He provided the means for the event to that place.

There is a moment on the stage where the dragon is pleased with Jesus nailed to the cross. The ground rumbles, the lights go out, and the sky turns black. The scene becomes silent and empty for three full days, and with the dawn of the next day, the lights lit the stage with a new light, Christ's victory over sin and death. As a result, the battle commences in Heaven, and the dragon and his followers are cast down to earth. "I saw Satan fall like lightning from heaven." (Luke 10:18 NIV)

Here, we have a dramatic ending to a glorious scene. The King of kings ascends to Heaven in Victory, while his nemesis falls in defeat to Earth. The Heavenly host celebrates victory and gives praise to God. The curtain closes on the scene in Heaven with an angel saying, "But woe to you, O earth and sea, for the devil has come down to you in great wrath because he knows that his time is short!" Satan knows his time is short, so he is more determined to take what is not his and destroy all humanity.

Christ's crucifixion defeats sin and death and gives strength to the angels in Heaven, for the victory is spiritual. They can rejoice and proclaim, "Now the salvation and the power and the kingdom of our God and the authority of His Christ have come, for the accuser of our brothers has been thrown down." Heaven is renewed and free of evil, so the angels celebrate God's victory.

However, it is woe for the Earth because Satan and his army are now among us; Satan and his minions are not in hell as often taught. Things will get worse for humanity. The setting for this action now takes place back on Earth. Here on earth, the supervillain and his mob of tugs have a different form. Their customs have changed to a transparent image. They seek to abide by some physical body to perform all kinds of wickedness. 'Come out of this man, you impure spirit!' (Mark 5:8 NIV) The Great Tribulation has begun. The battle continues on the three-dimensional planes of Earth. The dragon had lost access to the throne in Heaven and established his throne on Earth.

Here are clue cards that reveal a false concept and clarify a misunderstanding that Satan and his demons are in Hell. Also, wicked, non-believing people do not go to Hell when they die, not until the day of Judgement when God casts all evil into the lake of fire. Satan, the master of lies and deception, has convinced the world that he is in Hell, waiting for the wicked sinners. Hollywood has performed well in influencing the masses into this false teaching. Those views prevent anyone in modern society from believing that demon possession is possible. Science and atheism have made all forms of behavior a result of chemical unbalance in the brain or that certain types of people have different wiring. When, in fact, the demons are behind the so-called chemical unbalance and poor wiring. Today, we hear of people who identify with the gender inside them and not with their physical body.

The Supreme Director closes the curtain on angels in Heaven rejoicing and reopens it on Earth with fallen angels moving transparently among us. Therefore, this new scene is the first of many dealing with the segment in God's Drama called the Great Tribulation. It began when Christ rose from the dead, and Satan fell from Heaven, evening and morning of another day. Let's continue our review of Revelation.

13 "And when the dragon saw that he had been thrown down to the earth, he pursued the woman who had given birth to the male child. 14 But the woman was given two wings of the great eagle so that she might fly from the serpent into the wilderness, to the place where she is to be nourished for a time, and times, and half a time."

15 "The serpent poured water like a river out of his mouth after the woman, to sweep her away with a flood. 16 But the earth came to the help of the woman, and the earth opened its mouth and swallowed the river that the dragon had poured from his mouth."

17 "Then the dragon became furious with the woman and went off to make war on the rest of her offspring, on those who keep the commandments of God and hold to the testimony of Jesus. And he stood on the sand near the sea." We will see later that he sum-

mons a beast from the sea to do his dirty work. Notice her offspring, meaning her children and those who hold the testimony of her son Jesus.

Clue card review:

The Supreme Author uses poetic license to illustrate that shortly after Christ's Accession; the Villain tried to subdue the Mother of Christ with a flood that flowed from his mouth when the visual presentation is that of vomit blasphemies that issued from his mouth to stone the woman. Satan provokes the Jewish leaders to persecute the followers of Christ. They made claims that Mary was a prostitute. These same blasphemies continue in the Talmud to this very day. We can hear the evil Harlot singing the chorus, "Jesus was illegitimate and also conceived during the menstruation." The Talmud teaches that she was a prostitute, an adulteress, and therefore should die by stoning. The Quran refers to her seventy times and explicitly identifies her as the greatest of all women. The Quran refers to Mary more often than the New Testament.

She escapes and lives for three years on Mount Zion, followed by Bethany's three years, and for nine years near Ephesus. John took her there soon after the Jews had set Lazarus and his sisters Mary and Martha adrift upon the sea so that they should die at sea and the blood would not be on their hands. John had a house built for the Blessed Virgin outside Ephesus, where several Christian families and holy women had previously settled. Some lived in caves, others in the rocks, fitted with light woodwork to make dwellings, while others were in fragile huts or tents.

They had come here to escape violent persecution. The earth had opened her mouth and swallowed the voice of persecution by hiding Blessed Mary and others on the planet. Their dwellings were like hermits' cells, built by the refuges of what nature offered them. They lived apart from each other at a distance of a quarter of an hour. The whole settlement was like a scattered village so as not to draw attention. Mary's house was the only one built of stone.

From seats in the audience, we witness the mother who gave birth to the King of kings swiftly taken into hiding "underground" in the homes of both Jewish and Gentile believers of her son. While servants of the Harlot flood the streets, searching for the woman and her offspring. Also, those who keep the commandments of God and hold to the testimony of Jesus. The woman and child are persecuted by the Jewish Leader, the Harlot, who uses seduction and blasphemies to persuade both the people and the Romans that these Christian criminals need to be stopped and killed. In this scene enters a new character Saul, the persecutor of Christ believers, who becomes Paul, the defender of the Faith.

Since after the death and resurrection of Christ, the Pharisees, Sadducees, and Talmud Jews, with the support of atheists, through nearly two millenniums, to our present time have suggested that the disciples, during the decades following the death of Jesus, just invented the accounts. On stage, we see this group presented by a beautiful woman dressed in splendid clothing, with jewels of diamond and rubies, suggesting they stole the body and then claimed he rose from the dead. We also view the angry dragon pursuing the believers, with the help of the Harlot, the religious leaders of Judea, who socially slander the believers to provoke hatred to stone and kill Christ believers. Saul of Tarsus is one of them.

As the drama unfolds, we witness these Gospel critics saying that the disciples, in an attempt to enhance His authority, published a story that Jesus claimed to be God and resurrected from the dead. We hear that any fair-minded reader would consider these statements watered with deception pouring from Satan's mouth. In this drama, we have a comedy moment where Satan blames the believers for deceit through the Harlot.

With the help of the Harlot, the action continues as the Dragon tracks down the leaders of Christ's Church. The apostles are continually being threatened and pressured to deny their Lord during their ministry, especially as they face torture and martyrdom. We sit on the edge of our seats as none of these men chose to save their lives by denying their faith in Jesus. We hear a narrator ask, "Why would any individual risk being tortured and put to death for a lie?" In this act, the Dragon appears to be having the upper hand. His demon-possessed children of the Harlot precede to extinguish the leaders of the Church. We have not one but more than dozens who prefer to die rather than deny their testimony about Jesus Christ. Satan desires to kill Christ's disciples and put an end to the movement, but the campaign continues to grow.

We witness all of the cruel methods that Satan uses to inspire his minions to perform. Yet, these believers in Jesus persisted to the very end. The series of executions begins. Matthew suffered martyrdom in Ethiopia, killed by a sword wound. Mark dies in Alexandria, Egypt, after being dragged by horses through the streets. Luke suffers hanging in Greece as a result of his tremendous preaching to the lost. Peter was crucified upside down on a cross because he told his tormentors that he felt unworthy to die in the same way that Jesus Christ had died.

James the Just, the church leader in Jerusalem, was thrown over a hundred feet drop from the Temple's southeast pinnacle when he refused to deny his faith in Christ. When they discovered that he survived the fall, his enemies beat James to death with a club. It was the same pinnacle where Satan had taken Jesus during the Temptation.

James the Greater, a son of Zebedee, was a fisherman by trade and a strong church leader; James was ultimately beheaded in Jerusalem. The Roman officer who guarded James witnessed as James defended his faith at his trial. The officer was so amazed while walking beside James to the place of execution that conviction overcame him. Nevertheless, he declared his new faith to the judge, knelt beside James, and accepted beheading as a Christian.

Bartholomew, also known as Nathaniel, was a missionary to Asia Minor. He witnessed to our Lord in what is present-day Turkey. Bartholomew became martyred for his preaching in Armenia. He is believed to have been flayed to death by a whip. And perhaps he may have also been crucified.

Peter's brother Andrew also suffers crucifixion on a cross in Patras, Greece. He was first whipped severely by seven soldiers. Afterward, they tied his body to the cross with cords to prolong his agony. His followers witnessed and reported when he was walking toward the cross, Andrew saluted it in these words: "I have long desired and expected this happy hour. The cross has been consecrated by the body of Christ hanging on it." He continued to preach to his tormentors for two days until he expired. It is a great example: if the sacrifice and resurrection of Jesus were a lie, why would he permit this to happen to him and continue to preach?

Thomas was stabbed with a spear in India during one of his missionary trips to establish a church. Jude, the brother of Jesus, was killed with arrows when he refused to deny his faith in Christ.

Philip and his sister Mariamne, together with Bartholomew, preached in Greece, Phrygia, and Syria. He was martyred in Hierapolis when he was crucified.

One tradition maintains that the Apostle Matthias, who replaced Judas Iscariot with the Apostles, suffered death by stoning and beheading at the Jews' hands in Jerusalem.

Barnabas had traveled with Paul, and one of the seventy disciples wrote the Epistle of Barnabas. He preached throughout Italy and Cyprus. Barnabas died of stoning to death at Salonica. Phillip was crucified, according to the plaque in the church of the Holy Apostles.

Tradition holds that Paul was tortured and then beheaded by the evil Emperor Nero in Rome in AD 67. Paul had also survived being stoned, beaten with sticks, and drowning. In Rome, he endured a lengthy imprisonment, which allowed him to write his many epistles to the churches he had formed throughout the Roman Empire, mainly in Asia Minor today's Turkey. His letters have taught many of the foundational doctrines of Christianity. They also include a significant portion of the New Testament. Most scholars believe that Paul was released from house arrest in Rome in 62 AD and that he may have made a fourth missionary journey, as far as Spain, since it was his desire. (Rom 15:24, 28)

As we witness through our reading, these men did not sacrifice their lives for a lie. Instead, they testify to the truth that God sent His only Son to die for the sins of humankind. Christ's sacrifice over sin and death provides added strength to the angels in Heaven. It enables Michael and his angels to cast out Satan, the Dragon, and a third of the angels, now referred to as demons, are removed from Heaven. They are among us on earth to devour all of humanity. Satan has lost a battle in Heaven, has become furious with Mary, the Mother of Christ, and pursued her to kill her. Mary's offspring, meaning her children and those who keep the commandments of God and hold to the testimony of Jesus Christ, were now enemies of Satan, the Dragon.

We read in Galatians 3:26, "So in Christ Jesus, you are all children of God through faith." Therefore, through faith, we are also the offspring of Mary, the

Mother of Jesus Christ. John 19:26 When Jesus saw His Mother and the disciple he loved standing nearby, he said to her, "Woman, here is your son." Hence all who have faith in Jesus Christ are offspring of this woman and enemies of Satan, the Dragon who desires to exterminate her children. Through faith, this act of Motherhood is similar to Abram in Genesis 17:5 'No longer will you be called Abram; your name will be Abraham, for I have made you a father of many nations.' In Romans 4:16, we read. "Therefore, the promise comes by faith, so that it may be by grace and may be guaranteed to all Abraham's offspring-- not only to those who are of the law but also to those who have the faith of Abraham. He is the father of us all." Through his faith, he becomes the father of many nations. So it is with Mary that her faith and the love of God made her acceptable to be the Mother of Christ. Hence, she becomes the Mother of all.

There is also a shift to calling this woman the church, but a church is a collection of people. The church is the Bride of Christ. An offspring in the Eyes of God, one does not marry His mother. Therefore, the women in Chapter 12 can only be Jesus Christ's physical mother. Also, John is the very person who became the son of Mary by Christ's decree. (John 19:26)

The action contained in chapter 12 would have been history, past tense for John. Instead, it is a summary of his gospel, with the added activity of the nemesis of man. However, it is in both a literal and symbolic form, with the dragon's combined display and motivation. It clarifies Satan's present home and his followers, removing Satan's false notion of being in Hell, a deception he wants you to believe. It provides more exceptional ability and opportunity to deceive if you think he isn't nearby. It also confirms the present position of Mary, the Mother of Jesus Christ.

A note for the audience: the complete saga from the first line in Genesis to the last line in Revelation is Interactive Theatre. In the theatre or not, you are a part of the performance; there is no escape from refusing to perform or no belief in the saga. The result for inactive participation is the same as being an active supporter of the nemesis, a doomed member of the Dragon's followers.

As you experience the action of chapter 12 first, you have a brief history of the birth and successful mission of Jesus Christ and the fury of the Dragon. Evil began with Lucifer's desire to overthrow God from His Throne. Satan, with his envy, causes dissension and rebellion among the various ranks of angels. Even when Heaven returns to its righteous condition because of Christ's sacrifice, the angels rejoice. However, the restoration of the earth and humankind is still under Lucifer the Dragon's control.

John, the secretary of Revelation, the final book in God's Drama, faced martyrdom when placed in a vast basin of boiling oil during a wave of persecution in Rome. However, he was miraculously delivered from death when the oil became warm water. As a result, a rumor spread that he would not die, so John was sentenced to the mines on Patmos's prison island. It is where he recorded this prophetic Book of Revelation on Patmos. The apostle John was later freed and returned to serve as Bishop of Edessa in modern Turkey. He died as an older man, the only apostle to die peacefully. Therefore, John had already heard from those who witnessed that his fellow apostles had undergone execution along with his disciples. For John, the Great Tribulation had already begun before the time of the writing of Revelation. The destruction of the Temple and Jerusalem took place nearly 20 to 25 years before recording God's Revelation.

As an active participant in the Interactive Theatre presentation, you also have a costume to wear and a role to play. Regardless of the medium used or not used, you are a performer in God's Drama; no one can escape performing and not being judged on one's performance. Therefore, it is essential that you understand your role and how to act in the Drama.

Satan, with his followers, realizes their time is short. It means that God's wrath is sure to come, and it is happening. Satan, instead of admitting defeat and repenting of his crimes, continues a reign of terror. His jealousy and his desire for power have blinded his judgment. Since Jesus defeated him as a man, his anger toward humankind has magnified. It is the reason we are to put on the armor of God. The uniform the Lord has designed for those who choose to do battle, for, and with the Lord.

In a prior episode, we, the Interactive audience, were instructed to put on battle armor. Ephesians 6:14-18 (NIV) states 14 "Stand firm then, with the belt of truth buckled around your waist, with the breastplate of righteousness in place, 15 and with your feet fitted with the readiness that comes from the gospel of peace. 16 In addition to all this, take up the shield of faith, with which you can extinguish all the flaming arrows of the evil one. 17 Take the helmet of salvation and the sword of the Spirit, which is the word of God. 18 And pray in the Spirit on all occasions with all kinds of prayers and requests. With this in mind, be alert and always keep on praying for all the Lord's people". While the drama plays out, the Supreme Author includes instructions for the audience because the whole world is a part of God's stage. Since the Heavenly Host cast the Dragon and his army down to earth, we must now be ready to battle in both the physical and spiritual worlds. In Ephesians 6:12 (NLT), we read, "For we are not fighting against flesh-and-blood enemies, but against evil rulers and authorities of the unseen world, against mighty powers in this dark world, and against evil spirits in the heavenly places." Since the Dragon's fall, they are no longer in heavenly places. Please note that Paul is telling the community at Ephesus a similar announcement that the Dragon and his army are among them, also that this is one of the seven cities. Paul was preparing them to do battle against evil. When Chapter 12 begins, it becomes the prelude to the letters of the seven churches and Revelation events that follow.

Dragon's Early Fury
The years between the fall and the writing

We enter the theatre and glance at a playbill. We learn that the dragon has become active, and the "Great Tribulation" has begun with several significant events before recording the visions in Revelation. We open the playbill to read Excerpts from Josephus, the Jewish historian. He reports that a specific incredible phenomenon appeared in the sky a few days after the feast of Pentecost, on the one and twentieth day of Artemisius (May or June). Some people who saw an event occur stated before sun-setting, chariots and troops of soldiers in their armor running around the clouds and surrounding the cities. The dragon and his army had come to Jerusalem, having been exiled from Heaven.

A curtain opens, and a screen turns on; we see the madness in the city of Jerusalem. The leaders have put Jesus Christ to death and seek his followers, claiming that stealing the body to say it has risen.

Many followers of Christ become martyred until Ananus, the Chief Priest, orders James's stoning, the leader of the Church in Jerusalem. In turn, he receives his reward by being butchered in the heart of Jerusalem by Zealots, who claim the wealthy priest is a traitor. The High Priests had authority over the Temple worship and often acted as representatives of the Jews in dealing with the Roman occupation government. They had an interest in maintaining peace, some of them sincerely for the nation's good, while others no doubt had other motives to protect their wealth and power. The Zealots were ready to make Jesus King, but for their own purposes. They desired freedom from the Romans and felt the Priesthood stood in their way. As a result, many revolutionaries, especially the most radical group, the Zealots, considered their priests the enemy.

The Dragon and his army's spirit presence began provoking robbers to go into the city as if they were worshiping God. At the same time, they had daggers hidden under their garments, and mingling among the multitude, they slew Jonathan, another of the high priests. Since they never avenge the murder, the robbers gain confidence, go with the most exceptional security to the festivals, and have weapons concealed as done before. While mingling with the crowd, they eliminated their enemies. They are also dutifully employing other men for money, paid assassins that killed others in remote parts of the city and the Temple. They had the boldness to murder men anywhere without thinking of the impiety or consequence of their guilt. It sounds a lot like what radical Islam is doing today all around the globe.

Satan's anger against God is hardened further, so he desires to destroy God's Temple while establishing his exiled kingdom on earth. The master villain never imagines that he is only able to perform what God has already permitted. God has already scripted the Temple to destruction. There is no further need for the Temple and Temple sacrifice since Jesus Christ has provided the ultimate sacrifice for God. Now, God dwells through the Holy Spirit in the hearts of believers in Christ. Thus, Satan unknowingly performs God's Will, destroying the Temple.

In the darkness of night, the offspring of Esau, the Idumaeans, arrive. They scale through the city to the Temple. Evil enjoys the pleasure of darkness, for its spirit is but a shadow, and it has its origin in darkness. The Zealots are excited and, with high expectations, already positioned in the dark. They join forces with the Idumaeans, and together they boldly attack the guards; and those that stood watch, they killed those as they slept; but as those woke and cried out, the whole multitude arose and, in their amazement, seized hold of their weapons and immediately began their defense. The two murdering groups did not spare anyone, but their swords butchered to pieces, all they encountered. They gave no mercy to those who begged and stated their kinship. The guards, having no place for flight nor any hope for preservation, are cut to pieces one upon another in mounds. The remaining guards made their way into the city to avoid being slaughtered, only to face more miserable destruction. The outer Temple became overflowing with blood, and as the day dawned, the light shined on eight thousand five hundred dead bodies: Evening and Morning, the Slaughter of the Guards.

The guards of the Temple had taken Jesus Christ as a prisoner in the dead of night. Evil had taken Jesus during the night, and now corruption took the guards at night. So God uses the madness of Satan's fury to punish the priests and the guards of the Temple. God is saying; you killed My Son and His followers; now, here is your reward.

The dragon and his army had taken possession of the group's hearts and minds that called themselves Zealots. They became more wicked than those before the flood. The barbarity they comment on is seen by not granting burial to those slain in the city or those lying dead along the roads' side. In their hearts, they had agreed to cancel the laws of their country, the laws of nature, and those of God, at the same time that they defiled men with their evil actions. They would pollute Heaven itself, as the dragon had done. They left the dead bodies to rot in the heat of the sun. We see this very same behavior performed today by many who share the same ancestry DNA.

With their hedges down (Job 1:10), we see these men having welcomed the demons into their souls. Therefore, they trampled upon all the laws of man and laughed at the Laws of God, ignored the prophets, and ridiculed them as the tricks of jugglers. The same prophets foretold the many things concerning virtue and vice by their transgressions; the Zealots fulfilled those very prophecies belonging to Jerusalem. The city was now occupied, and the sanctuary was burnt by the right of war. When a revolution should invade the nation of Jews by their own hands should pollute the Temple of God. With their authority, the leaders rejected a living temple for an idol building and made it a stumbling block for the nation. As we witness the events that take place before the recording of Revelation, we are astonished by the workings of God's law of retribution.

Through the sedition of the Pharisees' harlot and members, they destroyed the living Temple of God, His Son. The irony is the very force behind the Pharisee and the Sadducee, who had, out of fear of losing control and wealth, chosen to reject and kill Christ, now suffer from the same evil power, as for why God permits the destruction of the Temple. It was only to be a foreshadowing of the living Temple and the minor sacrifice to that of the ultimate sacrifice of Jesus Christ. Therefore it was no longer needed. Also, in some ways, the Temple had become an idol of their worship. Thus, the Lamb of God has made the only sacrifice required for the forgiveness of sin.

We see on the screen comes to an event from 69 AD. A rebellion breaks out in Jerusalem. We know the dragon, the master of all villains, along with his army of thugs during the night while the Zealots slept; his forces planted the visions in their dreams to kill everyone who would oppose them. The Zealots, with their senses aroused for blood, begin their rebellion. As a result, Rome sent an enormous army under the command of Vespasian to retake Judea. The Roman military quickly subdued the Jewish forces in Galilee and laid siege to Jerusalem. Vespasian received an order to return to Rome, and the siege was continued by his son, Titus. He builds a wall around the city and begins to starve the inhabitants. Once the rebellion was weak by starvation, Titus captured Jerusalem on Ab's ninth day in 70 AD (according to the Jewish calendar). He burned the Temple and Jerusalem, killing or selling into slavery tens of thousands of Jews. Titus destroyed The Second Temple on the same day that Babylon destroyed the first. As Jesus left the temple and walked away, His disciples came up to Him to point out its building. 2 "Do you see all these things?" He replied. "Truly I tell you, not one stone here will be left on another; everyone will be toppled." (Matt 24:1-2 NIV)

The scene on the screen is 73 AD after the fall of Jerusalem. Jewish Zealots managed to hold out at the Fortress of Masada for three years as they continued to oppose Rome; Masada's location is in the Desert of Judaea, near the Dead Sea's shores. The Romans prevented food supplies from entering Masada as they had done in Jerusalem. When it became clear, through starvation, that they could hold out no longer, Masada's defenders committed mass suicide rather than become captives of the Romans. Here, in this scene, we view the irony of the Jewish people.
They did nothing to save their Messiah, and now they cannot protect themselves, and rather than die a hero's death, they choose suicide. When I wrote this, I heard the Still Small Voice say, "I ordered that they would die by their own hand."

The scene changes again this time; the place is in Italy in the decadent, promiscuous city of Pompeii and Herculaneum, where prostitution and homosexuality are the order of the day. We view this scene because God also punishes the immorality of the Gentiles. In 79AD, Mount Vesuvius erupted, destroying two cities. Most of the cities' populations managed to flee, but 20,000 inhabitants died. Also, we witness the wickedness of man when inspired by Satan. Vespasian ordered the Colosseum built a year later, but it fell to his son Titus to dedicate it. The Colosseum provided the Romans with a new form of entertainment, the deadly sport of gladiator games, which became their main attraction; however, watching lions eating Christians became part of their enjoyment. Colosseum used gladiator games until 404 AD. Today, we view killing in films and video games as the same form of entertainment.

Emperor Domitian succeeds his older brother Titus and commences a reign of terror after an abortive coup against him. Domitians levied heavy taxes on the provinces, mainly Jewish and Christian faiths, refusing to worship other Romans. Today, Islam does the same to those who wish to live and not worship as they do. Domitian assassination was in 96 AD, just around the time of the writing of Revelation. So we see John on the Island of Patmos writing.

Cue Card Review:

Our playbill provides additional information, perhaps why the Lord does not tell John to write a letter to Rome, Alexandria, Jerusalem, Galatia, Antioch, Colossians, or Thessalonica, seven other major cities of the Roman Empire. One needs to ask why Jesus excluded Rome and the other cities since the Christians would experience the same fate, if not worse treatment, than in the other seven cities that receive a letter. Domitian has placed heavy taxes on them with consequences for not paying. The answer is in their persecution and martyred, whereas the others were not, and they are outside of the setting of Babylonia.

While sitting off stage with my laptop on a small table, meditating on my role in God's Drama, I wondered what could be the reason for being absent from the list of churches. One reason for not writing is number seven. It is God's number for completeness. Seven twice would seem to indicate a higher degree. Another possible reason came to mind. All of the seven churches John writes are near one another, while the others are not. When we look at Rome, we know that Nero blamed them for the burning of Rome. We know that Caesar's Worship would be more there than anywhere else. We know that Christians became a form of Roman entertainment, being food for hungry lions. Yet, Jesus does not have John write a warning or a blessing to those at the church of Rome. Didn't the Christians holding fast in Rome deserve a blessing?

We also know that both Peter and Paul die there. Two essential leaders of the early church, John does not write a word to the other churches they founded. Most theologians refer to Rome as the home of the Anti-Christ, Rome for the False Prophet, and finally Rome as the Harlot. My mind questions this possibility. The Supreme Author left them out of the drama because Rome and the others do not play a significant role that many incorrectly interpret.

I prayed and meditated; I asked God why He neglected to warn His faithful followers in Rome and the other cities not mentioned. I asked, "Are they so evil to even curse or make any reference to spitting them out?" You would think that if the unholy trinity were coming out of Rome, the followers in Rome would have received a letter with a warning like the others to hold fast and to be able to spot Satan when he comes. Also, two of his most celebrated followers die a martyr's death there. There had to be a faithful church in Rome that could have loved to be encouraged by Jesus. There is no letter to the church in Jerusalem since Titus, the Roman General, destroyed the city in 71AD. Nor did any of the other communities in the Roman Empire.

The idea just kept coming; God and Christ must have had a reason for having John write to the seven churches in Asia Minor. The evidence did not support the notion that Rome was evil and, therefore, no letter. All seven cities are in modern-day Turkey. All seven cities are a part of the Eastern portion of the Roman Empire. They were all part of a significant trade route, which was why Constantine moved Rome's capital to Asia Minor, today's Turkey, in the first place since they are all part of a trade route that resembles a lamp-stand with seven candles on one stand. Seven cities on a single trade route. It is here where Satan the Dragon has made his home. Revelation tells us where the throne of Satan is, and it is not in Italy. All seven churches are in the ancient Kingdom of Babylon. The evidence does not support the idea of Rome. It can only be an error or nothing more than false teaching, just what Jesus warns. As we journey through Revelation, the nation that was, is not, and now is will become clear.

Thus, it became common in the first century to equate Rome with the final empire of Edom. However, the Ottoman Empire followed Rome and could have been the feet while Rome was the legs. Since the Ottoman Empire, the faith in Babylon's area is Islam, and they refer to their ancestry as Ishmael and possibly also Esau. These two tribes would make up the empire of Edom. Keeping this line of thinking, Turkey, Syria, Iran, Iraq, and Egypt are five nations with Shiite and Sunni groups. Therefore, we have two groups of five or two feet with five toes of Nebuchadnezzar's statue from his dream before the rock is thrown and destroys the statue.

We have set the stage between the Ascension of Christ and the casting out of the Dragon. Until the recording of Revelation has been laid out for the foundation of the final acts of the concluding episode of God's Drama. The very first sentence is, 'The Revelation of Jesus Christ, which God gave him to show to his servants the things that must soon take place.' God has Jesus revealed to John the things that are soon to take place. So, the idea that Jesus tells John to write to each of the seven churches about some symbolic future, with each church at a different period in the church's history, is contrary to God's statement through Christ. The phrase soon to take place is just that. I have read some theologians wishing to claim symbolic churches. The letters reveal the community's present condition and their possible future.

When we compare them with the letters written by Paul, we discern and observe the same conditions. Therefore, the seven church events are not various stages of the church but events taking place then. These same conditions have been present throughout the ages, and as in the past, they can all take place in one community simultaneously. Also, keep in mind that Satan is now on earth with his demon army. He will get busy deceiving humanity into Satan worship, with all forms of sensual pleasure, and those who refuse that Satan kills or makes life a living hell, so they blame God.

As I mentioned, the letters' format is similar to that of the letters written by Paul. We have the intro, the writer to the recipient, followed by a blessing and acknowledgment of the Lord Jesus Christ. Next, there is an acknowledgment of approval and disapproval, with instruction and warning. Each letter can stand alone and is not written in symbolic form but is literal. They would each be going to a different recipient with a private message for each of them. Suggesting anything other is false doctrine. Yes, all seven churches may have read another church's letters for additional information on moral behavior, but each letter has a specific recipient.

Jesus wants these churches to know about the events that will take place at a later date. "But about that day or hour, no one knows, not even the angels in heaven, nor the Son, but only the Father." (Mark 13:32). Jesus knows what will happen and where it will happen, but not when it will happen; therefore, Christ is warning those most affected by the events. As we journey through Revelation, it will become clear that the focus is on Asia Minor, the six nations that presently make up the Babylonian Empire's territory. They are Egypt, Syria, Turkey, Iran, Iraq, and Israel. Now, we are ready to take a journey with John. As we read John's narration and visualize the images, you are there with him and take particular notice of the tone in which Jesus speaks. God often uses a similar tone of voice when speaking to Moses in Leviticus and in Numbers, where God gives instruction and reprimand.

The Letters provide a reprimand, a warning of what will happen as a result of disobedience. I will show that history does show what happens to these seven church communities. It will also provide a clue as to why Rome does not receive a letter.

Seven Churches
Greetings and Doxology

4 John to the seven churches that are in Asia: "Grace to you and peace from Him who is and who was and who is to come, and from the seven spirits who are before His Throne, 5 and from Jesus Christ the faithful witness, the firstborn of the dead, and the ruler of kings on earth. To Him who loves us and has freed us from our sins by His blood 6 and made us a kingdom of priests to His God and Father, to Him be glory and dominion forever and ever. Amen. 7 Behold, He is coming with the clouds, and every eye will see Him, even those who pierced Him, and all tribes of the earth will wail on account of Him. Even so, Amen."

8 "I am the Alpha and the Omega," says the Lord God, "who is and who was and who is to come, the Almighty."

Vision of the Son of Man

10 "I was in the Spirit on the Lord's day, and I heard behind me a loud voice like a trumpet 11 saying,

'Write what you see in a book and send it to the seven churches, to Ephesus, and to Smyrna and to Pergamum and to Thyatira and to Sardis and to Philadelphia and to Laodicea.'"

12 "Then I turned to see the voice that was speaking to me, and on turning, I saw seven golden lampstands, 13 and in the midst of the lampstands one like a Son of Man, clothed with a long robe and with a golden sash around his chest. 14 The hairs on his head were white, like white wool, like snow. His eyes were like a flame of fire, 15 his feet were like burnished bronze, refined in a furnace, and his voice was like the roar of many waters. 16 In his right hand, he held seven stars; from his mouth came a sharp two-edged sword, and his face was like the sun shining in full strength."

17 "When I saw him, I fell at his feet as though dead. But he laid his right hand on me, saying, 'Fear not, I am the first and the last, 18 and the living one. I died, and behold, I am alive forevermore, and I have the keys of Death and Hades. 19 Write, therefore, the things that you have seen, those that are, and those that are to take place after this. 20 As for the mystery of the seven stars that you saw in my right hand, and the seven golden lampstands, the seven stars are the angels of the seven churches, and the seven lampstands are the seven churches.'"

We are standing there with John, who knew Jesus; he had traveled with Christ for a time, times, and a half time, but here we see John fear the images before him. This picture would frighten me; a man with a sword coming out of his mouth would be terrifying.

However, realizing the symbolic description of Jesus Christ, we sense that His eyes are red with fire, indicating He is angry and is about to deal with evil. His words, His orders cut like a knife and kill. We quickly realize that someone who could heal the sick, make the blind see and crippled walk, and raise Lazarus from the dead can also rapidly say die, and we learn the meaning of fearing the Lord God. Our mind speaks to us, "Yes, His tongue is a two-edged sword because He has the power to command over life or death."

We hear Jesus, who died and is alive forever, tell John to write down those things he has seen: past tense, those that are present, and those that are to take place in the future. Therefore, Revelation's events are past, present, and future, as of John's writing. We must realize that many of the occurrences that John beheld for the future may well be in our distant past. We can sense from the look in the Lord's eyes that Christ is upset with each church. Each letter is specific for a particular community of believers; however, be aware that the same blessings and curses hold literal for us in our own time. God the Father is the same yesterday as today and tomorrow. The same fate is ours if we live as those of the past.

To the Church in Ephesus

(2) "To the angel of the church in Ephesus write: 'The words of him who holds the seven stars in his right hand, who walks among the seven golden Lamp Stands.'"

2 "I know your works, your toil, and your patient endurance, and how you cannot bear with those who are evil but have tested those who call themselves apostles and are not, and found them to be false. 3 I know you are enduring patiently and bearing up for my name's sake, and you have not grown weary. 4 But I have this against you, that you have abandoned the love you had at first. 5 Remember therefore from where you have fallen; repent, and do the works you did at first. If not, I will come to you and remove your lampstand from its place unless you repent."

While listening to Christ speak to John, we recall in Ephesians 4:17 (NIV) the Epistle of Paul giving this same church the following instructions. "So I tell you this, and insist on it in the Lord, that you must no longer live as the Gentiles do, in the futility of their thinking. 18 They are darkened in their understanding and separated from the life of God because of the ignorance that is in them due to the hardening of their hearts. 19 Having lost all sensitivity, they have given themselves over to sensuality to indulge in every kind of impurity, and they are full of greed."

We perceive that Paul provides this instruction is because he fears that they will return to their old ways. The Ephesians had worshiped the god Artemis and her idols. Paul's concern was that they would return to their former lifestyle. Jesus here says you have abandoned the love you had at first for me and returned to your previous lifestyle. Christ has just given instructions and a warning to repent and to do the works you once did. It happens even today. Let us continue our journey through Revelation and this letter to Ephesus.

6 "Yet this you have: you hate the works of the Nicolaitans, which I also hate. 7 He who has an ear, let him hear what the Spirit says to the churches. To the one who conquers, I will grant to eat of the tree of life, which is in the paradise of God." The Nicolaitans worship a false god. The false God is always Satan; he deceives individuals into worshiping an idol other than God and Christ, and in this manner, you worship him.

We read again the line, 'what the Spirit says to the churches.' Dwelling on the word churches, John wrote churches so that the messages were for all seven, but it must also be for more than those seven churches because we can quickly fall back on old habits. Reading the history of this city, we ask ourselves, was it more or less evil than Rome, and what future would the city of Ephesus have? Christ said, unless you repent, I will remove my lamp stand. Many believers died. History shows it was conquered many times until abandoned by the 16th century. The fact that Ephesus is gone would indicate Christ removed His Lamp Stand, meaning he removed His light, His Spirit, from Ephesus. Rome is still here. Should that be a reason to always point to Rome? When Jesus Christ punished this city, would He not punish others, including Rome?

To the Church in Smyrna

8 "And to the angel of the church in Smyrna write: 'The words of the first and the last, who died and came to life.'"

9 "I know your tribulation and your poverty (but you are rich) and the slander of those who say that they are Jews and are not but are a synagogue of Satan. 10 Do not fear what you are about to suffer. Behold, the devil is about to throw some of you into prison, that you may be tested, and for ten days, you will have tribulation. Be faithful unto death, and I will give you the crown of life. 11 He who has an ear, let him hear what the Spirit says to the churches. The one who conquers will not be hurt by the second death."

It is easy for us to see that their poverty is in their Spirit, and their riches are of the world. In the letter to the Romans, 2:28, Paul wrote, "A person is not a Jew who is one only outwardly, nor is circumcision merely outward and physical. 29 No, a person is a Jew who is one inwardly, and circumcision is circumcision of the heart, by the Spirit, not by the written code. Such a person's praise is not from other people but God." Paul's position is that those who live by faith have their hearts circumcised, making all Christians, regardless of their ethnic background, considered Jews, spiritually speaking children of Abraham. Jesus tells us in Matthew 6:1, "Be careful not to perform your righteous acts before men to be seen by them. If you do, you will have no reward from your Father in Heaven. 2 So when you give to the needy, do not sound a trumpet before you, as the hypocrites do in the synagogues and on the streets, to be praised by men. Truly, I tell you, they already have their reward."

These people are only abundant in their outward appearance. How often do we hear preachers with an abundance of messages? Notice here that Jesus Christ continues to refer to those who claim to be

Jews and are not, and they are a synagogue of Satan. Matthew 23:33 Jesus called them a brood of vipers. The Jewish leaders rejected Jesus for their wealth and caused the messes to stumble and plummet as well, just as their Father, the dragon, prompted a third of the angels to fall. Paul also makes remarks about forcing Gentiles to follow the law instead of believing through faith. Here, we have a group of people who are more concerned with outward appearance than actual belief. Today we have Jewish people who stand to face a wall to pray. Is this not a form of display and idolatry? "But when you pray, go into your room, close the door, and pray to your unseen Father. Then your Father, who sees what is done in secret, will reward you." (Matt: 6:6 NIV)

So we have Smyrna falling to false teaching. Here, we have Jesus calling the Jews a synagogue of Satan worshipers and that the believers are to suffer being placed in prison by those who claim to be Jews. Today, we have Zionists, and those who follow the Talmud, even persecute Jews that abide by the Torah, so are they Jews or something else, a synagogue of Satan? Is this taking place today when we hear of Liberal media slandering Christians? The same group disparaged and persecuted first Christ and then His followers. What I find interesting is the number of Israelites God destroyed just a short time after having left Egypt. For opposing Moses, even Aaron and Miriam oppose Moses, their brother. Moses' sister receives punishment for seven days with leprosy. (Number 12:10 NIV) If Moses had not interceded for her, she would have remained that way. Exodus, Leviticus, and Numbers have several events where individuals, families, groups, and even thousands are swapped away (killed) due to their disobedience, lack of faith, and trust in God.

To the Church in Pergamum

12 "And to the angel of the church in Pergamum write: The words of him who has the sharp two-edged sword."

13 "I know where you dwell, where Satan's throne is. Yet you hold fast my name, and you did not deny my faith even in the days of Antipas my faithful witness, who was killed among you, where Satan dwells. 14 But I have a few things against you: you have some there who hold the teaching of Balaam, who taught Balak to put a stumbling block before the sons of Israel so that they might eat food sacrificed to idols and practice sexual immorality. 15 So also you have some who hold the teaching of the Nicolaitans. 16 Therefore repent. If not, I will come to you soon and war against them with the sword of my mouth. 17 He who has an ear, let him hear what the Spirit says to the churches. To the one who conquers, I will give some of the hidden manna, and I will give him a white stone with a new name written on the stone that no one knows except the one who receives it."

As we watch and listen to this performance, we hear Jesus say that Satan's throne is in Pergamum, and it is the place where he dwells. Jesus said it. Therefore it must be. Some wish to think that the Pergamon Altar is the throne of Satan, a monumental construction built during the reign of Greek King Eumenes II in the first half of the second century BC. The throne's structure is one of the terraces of the Acropolis of Pergamon's ancient Greek City in Asia Minor, today's Turkey. There is a severe problem with this point of view. Satan lives in the spirit world, and therefore, his throne is also in the spirit world and may look nothing like the throne to Zeus, built by human hands. Also, the meaning of the word 'throne' could mean the place where Satan rules.

Why all the continued pointing to Rome? The reason for this false teaching is the idea that Pergamum is symbolic of some future church. Once again, if the church in Rome is Satan's seat, then Jesus, being the Son of God, would have said it. After all, He warns Pergamum because it is there that Satan's throne rests, but Satan would have you believe that it is elsewhere to devise us. Jesus alerts us that Satan's throne is in Pergamum, Turkey. It is the seat of his earthly empire, the capital of his false, evil kingdom; from there, it branches out into the rest of the earth. Here in Asia Minor, Satan has created a false religion that practices all his forms of wickedness.

Today these seven churches are all located in Turkey, a nation with its belief in Islam that I find interesting. I never heard any theologian mention that the meat was a sacrifice to their God in Islam. It suggests that Balaam's practice taught Balak to put a stumbling block before the sons of Israel and Christians so that they might eat food sacrificed to idols and practice sexual immorality was present then and is still with us today. By eating food sacrificed to idols, an individual places a hole in the hedge of God's protection and lets a demon in. "Have you not put a hedge around him and his household and everything he has? You have blessed the work of his hands so that his flocks

and herds are spread throughout the land." (Job 1:10). When God removes the hedge, Satan can destroy everything that Job has, all but his life.
In our modern age of atheism, with its belief in science and false theories of evolution, we have arrived at the notion that behavior is a form of chemical unbalance in the human brain, and the idea of demon possession of any kind is pure nonsense. With all this science, the degree of hate and violence is increasing at an alarming rate. With its violent message, rap music has created a culture of hatred, with no reflection on their behavior and nature. People have permitted their hedges to welcome evil. Nowhere is this more prevalent than in Babylon, where we find the throne of Satan.

Islam, not Catholicism, since the seventh century, has taken on many wives, child brides, and even sex slaves. They also eat meat that is a sacrifice to a god and sell it in their stores. Roman Catholics do not conduct these practices. The so-called "born again" would have you believe that Catholics are not Christians. Many have not ever set foot inside a Catholic church and listened to the beauty of the worship of Jesus Christ.

Reflecting on history, one also needs to consider that the Angelo Church had slaves in America, not Roman Catholics. The Angelo Church began with Henry VIII because the Pope would not give him a divorce; sexual immorality and adultery were in the Angelo Church through the granting of a divorce. Still, they love to point the finger, forgetting to remove the log from their eye first. One needs to ask and research this question. Where is the city of Pergamum today? The answer is that it is gone with the removal of the Lamp Stand. However, Satan still dwells there. The same theologians will say that Satan's throne, a building, was moved to Germany and used by Hitler. However, Jesus tells us that Satan dwells in this city, Pergamum in Turkey, not in the Vatican in Rome or anywhere else.

There is one more new warning that Jesus gives to this Church, and that is He will come with a sword in His mouth and war against them if they do not repent. Later in this final episode of God's Drama, we read that Jesus comes riding a white horse with a two-edged sword in His mouth. Jesus has just stated that He is coming to Turkey.

To the Church in Thyatira

18 "And to the angel of the church in Thyatira write: 'The words of the Son of God, who has eyes like a flame of fire, and whose feet are like burnished bronze.'"

19 "I know your works, your love and faith and service, and patient endurance, and that your latter works exceed the first. 20 But I have this against you, that you tolerate that woman Jezebel, who calls herself a prophetess and is teaching and seducing my servants to practice sexual immorality and to eat food sacrificed to idols. 21 I gave her time to repent, but she refused to repent of her sexual immorality. 22 Behold, I will throw her onto a sickbed, and those who commit adultery with her I will throw into great tribulation unless they repent of her works, 23 and I will strike her children dead. And all the churches will

know that I am he who searches mind and heart, and I will give to each of you according to your works. 24 But to the rest of you in Thyatira, who do not hold this teaching, who have not learned what some call the deep things of Satan, to you I say, I do not lay on you any other burden. 25 Only hold fast what you have until I come. 26 The one who conquers and who keeps my works until the end, to him I will give authority over the nations, 27 and he will rule them with a rod of iron, as when earthen pots are broken in pieces, even as I myself have received authority from my Father. 28 And I will give him the morning star. 29 He who has an ear, let him hear what the Spirit says to the churches."

As we watch from our seats in the audience, we see that Jesus speaks to those in Thyatira and not some future period. This priestess was teaching the community of saints a satanic message, eating food sacrificed to idols, and the practice of sexual immorality. Also, we have Satan's profound things; this would be the teaching of black magic, the very thing that the Pharisees accuse Jesus of using to heal. In time, the people would become the children of a type of 'Jezebel' practicing this false teaching with a desire to spread the word with her evil. This practice still exists in the Kingdom of Babylon, today's Turkey, Syria, Iran, Iraq, and Egypt in the name of a false god.

Some in the audience may wonder about another teaching. One that suggests that eating the body of Christ is cannibalism. However, in John 6:53, Jesus said to them, "Very truly I tell you, unless you eat the flesh of the Son of Man and drink his blood, you have no life in you." Christians do not eat meat sacrificed to a false god; it is wrong to do so. Paul taught this message to the very same churches. However, the repeated practice that the Lord gave us at the Last Supper before His crucifixion is what we need to eat. It is a new covenant and a new form of manna. This community of believers stayed strong and stood fast. The City was home to a Christian community from Apostolic times until 1922, when the Greek Orthodox population was deported because of their Christian Faith. The bread of presence foreshadows the Eucharist. (Exodus 25:30)

To the Church in Sardis

(3) "And to the angel of the church in Sardis write: 'The words of him who has the seven spirits of God and the seven stars.'"

"'I know your works. You have the reputation of being alive, but you are dead. 2 Wake up and strengthen what remains and is about to die, for I have not found your works complete in the sight of my God. 3 Remember, then, what you received and heard. Keep it, and repent. If you will not wake up, I will come like a thief, and you will not know at what hour I will come against you. 4 Yet you have still a few names in Sardis, people who have not soiled their garments, and they will walk with me in white, for they are worthy. 5 The one who conquers will be clothed thus in white garments, and I will never blot his name out of the book of life. I will confess his name before my Father and before his angels. 6 He who has an ear, let him hear what the Spirit says to the churches.'"

Listening to the Lord dictating this letter, we understand this is a church of pretenders. Those people talk the talk but don't walk the walk. This church is much like Smyrna, dealing with outward appearances. They speak of things Christian, but in their hearts, they have no genuine belief. They put their faith in things, government, money, and other people, all while claiming to be Christians. They are like, "The seeds sprouted quickly because the soil was shallow. 6, But the plants soon wilted under the hot sun, and since they didn't have deep roots, they died." (Matt 13: 5-6 NIV) They died because they never developed a strong faith in Christ.

Sardis could be an example of many churches in America today. People who pretend to be alive in Christ but are dead. They speak about the Lord but are more concerned about themselves and their wealth and pleasure. The church leaders preach the abundance message to fatten their own pockets by making God the servant of man while spending little time teaching the real meaning of salvation. They call themselves 'born again Christians' while parading with an air of purity. They pretend to trust in the Lord and to have faith when, in fact, they only have trust and confidence in what they can touch with their hands.

We see this same practice with other religions that wear their faith's costumes for others to see. Therefore again, this ancient church is a model for many of today. By the 19th century, Sardis was in ruins; another Lamp Stand had gone dead because there was never real life. I often wonder how Christians in America and elsewhere can support political leaders who do not demonstrate nor promote Christian values. Instead, they support abortions and various forms of sexual immorality as an acceptable alternative lifestyle when they contradict Biblical truths. The people of Sardis, like many today, were and are hypocrites.

To the Church in Philadelphia

7 "And to the angel of the church in Philadelphia write: 'The words of the holy one, the true one, who has the key of David, who opens and no one will shut, who shuts and no one opens.'"

8 "I know your works. Behold, I have set before you an open door that no one is able to shut. I know that you have but little power, and yet you have kept my word and have not denied my name. 9 Behold, I will make those of the synagogue of Satan who say that they are Jews and are not, but lie—behold, I will make them come and bow down before your feet, and they will learn that I have loved you. 10 Because you have kept my word about patient endurance, I will keep you from the hour of trial that is coming on the whole world to try those who dwell on the earth. 11. I am coming soon. Hold fast to what you have so that no one may seize your crown. 12 The one who conquers, I will make him a pillar in the temple of my God. Never shall he go out of it, and I will write on him the name of my God, and the name of the city of my God, the new Jerusalem, which comes down from my God out of heaven, and MY own new name. 13 He who has an ear, let him hear what the Spirit says to the churches."

While we are part of this interactive theater and listening to Christ speak of His promises for those who endure to the end, it becomes uplifting and fills us with joy, and it gives us strength. This church is a representation of those who genuinely follow in Christ's footsteps. Now, we have a vital clue as to what is to develop. The first significant evidence is Satan's synagogue, which says that they are Jews and are not. Matthew 23:33, "You snakes! You brood of vipers! How will you escape being condemned to hell?" Jesus condemned the sovereignty of the day. Many of today's rabbis teach not from the Torah but the Talmud. The same accusations he faced when he spoke in the synagogue are expressed and taught about Him. Jesus uses the word synagogue, not the church. A fact ignored by many theologians. Today, these vipers are Zionists; just as in Christ's time, they are more concerned about a nation and power than God. Jesus blesses this church.

Again, Jesus suggests that He is coming soon. The early followers assumed Christ was returning in their generation because he said, "Truly I tell you, this generation will certainly not pass away until all these things have happened." (Matt 24:34 NIV) Hence, these members of the church were expecting this blessing to hold fast. Jesus did not come in that generation, but the promise is still valid for those to keep their faith and stand fast against evil. Watching him dictate to John, our impression is that he thought he was coming soon, and we recall He once said, "But about that day or hour no one knows, not even the angels in heaven, nor the Son, but only the Father" (Mark 13:32 NIV)

To the Church in Laodicean

14 "And to the angel of the church in Laodicean write: The words of the Amen, the faithful and true witness, the beginning of God's creation."

15 "I know your works: you are neither cold nor hot. Would that you were either cold or hot! 16 So, because you are lukewarm and neither hot nor cold, I will spit you out of my mouth. 17 For you say, I am rich, I have prospered, and I need nothing, not realizing that you are wretched, pitiable, poor, blind, and naked. 18 I counsel you to buy from me gold refined by fire, so that you may be rich, and white garments so that you may clothe yourself and the shame of your nakedness may not be seen, and salve to anoint your eyes, so that you may see. 19 Those whom I love, I reprove and discipline, so be zealous and repent. 20 Behold, I stand at the door and knock. If anyone hears my voice and opens the door, I will come into him and eat with him, and he with me. 21 The one who conquers, I will grant him to sit with me on my throne, as I also conquered and sat down with My Father on His Throne. 22 He who has an ear, let him hear what the Spirit says to the churches."

We know that an event like this did occur because Paul writes to Hebrews 5: 11-12, "We have much to say about this, but it is hard to make it clear to you because you no longer try to understand. Though you should be a teacher at this time, you need someone to teach you the elementary truths of God's Word all over again. You need milk, not solid food!" Here, we read that the people were lukewarm. These are the half-hearted followers of Christ. Those who have wealth care not of the things of the spirit, for they think they are blessed. They need to relearn the real things of value.

Each of the churches is not far from Satan's throne, so his influence is always there. We have read about eating meat sacrificed to a false god, sexual immorality, false teaching, and soft, half-hearted believers. All this takes place near the new capital of Rome, Istanbul, in Turkey, where the throne of Satan rests. We also read that the synagogue of Satan is there. All of these seven churches reveal some warring for us, for like other passages in the Bible, the Word of God is to instruct and lift our spirit. This church has become a titular see, a former diocese, and a church on paper only because of its lukewarm nature. We can assume Christ spit her out.

While watching Christ dictate to John, we heard Jesus give each of the churches warnings to stand fast or have their light burned out. The Holy Spirit, the Seven Spirits of God, would be removed. We read what was happening at those seven churches in Turkey and what they needed to do to prevail. Also, by examining history, we discovered the results of time. One does not require a divinity degree to read that the letter is literal. Our Lord is merely saying this is what I approve of, and this is what I disapprove of, and you need to stop doing it. I think that it is pretty straightforward if you ask me. Jesus is telling John to write to these churches, and they need to change during that first century.

These are not recommendations before He comes back; they are not separate periods of His church throughout history, as some theologians would like us to believe. They are the same type of reprimands that we read throughout Leviticus and Numbers. They are warnings and instructions for each of those churches. Most of those very same churches or communities are nothing more than a pile of rubble today. However, a city of Believers in Jesus Christ is still in Rome today.

I often praise my sons when they are doing an excellent job, and I tell them when they are not. I don't need a doctoral degree to know right from wrong. In the letters to the churches, Jesus Christ is merely giving us parental instruction. Anything beyond this is false teaching and a narcissistic behavior to show that they are brighter than the rest of us like Korah of Numbers chapter 16 wanting to dethrone Moses. Just as God made Moses His representative on earth, so did Christ make Peter.

The false teachers are doing the very same today. These seven letters deal with the events that were taking place during John's time. If you read Paul's letters, you will find that he expresses the same concerns and offers recommendations. The irony is that today's theologians create the various doctrines that Jesus and God would disapprove of by presenting a false interpretation.

What does all this mean for us today? Simple, we read the Gospels, the Letters of Paul, and other books of the Bible for instruction from events in the past. God and Jesus Christ give us a warning, and we need to listen and obey. From God's first warning in the Garden of Eden to the letters to the churches, humans past and present have failed to listen to God and have turned to Satan's voice; rebellion is more natural than obedience. Jesus said, "You will recognize them by their fruits." (Matt 7:16 ESV)

The curtain closes on the stage for a scene change from the Island of Patmos; there is a shift from John's present earth to the current state of Heaven, as it was then. We can all agree this event took place in John's lifetime. He saw it, and he wrote about it. We are about to read and examine the events that will take place in John's present and future, which indicate some of these proceedings are in our past, some are current, and others in our future.

Today, many Christians have grown soft and believe that God will plunk them from the earth when some terrible trouble and adversity arrives, but trials are always present. War, famine, killing, and disease are still ready to destroy us. We are to stand fast, to have perseverance, and not crumble in these times of trial. A Christian Warrior's mindset is no matter how badly the fighting goes; you continue to fight even when all is lost. Unlike those of Masada who choose suicide, then die at a Roman soldier's hand or become a slave. A Christian Warrior has orders from the Lord to stand fast to persevere to the last breath.

However, Jesus Christ, as I have already stated, did not tell John to write to the Church in Rome. All of the seven churches that Jesus sent a warning to had aspired to all forms of wickedness. While in Rome, every citizen sought the qualities of life known as Via Romana - the Roman Way. It is an ideal code of conduct for all people, and everyone should aspire to this way of life. These qualities gave the Roman Republic the moral strength to conquer and civilize the world. The most prolonged recorded period of peace on earth was under Pax Roman. Today many, if not all, of Via Romana's characteristics are the standards that we can measure our social behavior and character. Notice how many of these characteristics are also Christian virtues, and many of today's Television evangelists share these very same concepts in their prosperity messages. One must keep in mind that, just as in America today, the actions and behavior of the elite in power do not necessarily reflect the average citizen.

When you view these Roman citizens' components, you get a different picture than what some would like us to believe. You will see that many of the characteristics of the Roman citizen are also ideas shared by Christians. They are also the backbone of ideas and concepts that our forefathers of America created in our Republic. They model our system of governing after Rome. Rome was the first nation to be a Republic with a Senate that made laws, not a despot or a King. I am presenting this information to provide a backdrop of the lifestyle of the Roman citizen. What it was like at the time of the writing of the Book of Revelation. I will give the Latin term for these characteristics, followed by an English definition. I find it interesting that Paul writes this to the Romans. "Indeed, when Gentiles, who do not have the law, do by nature things required by the law, they are a law for themselves, even though they do not have the law." (Romans 2:14 NIV) Here are the Roman attributes.

Auctoritas - Spiritual Authority; the sense of one's social standing, built up through experience. In Christianity, this spiritual authority comes with unity with the Holy Spirit through Jesus Christ.

Comitas - Humor: Being able not to take things too seriously by having an ease of manner, courtesy, openness, friendliness, and hospitality.

Clementia - Mercy, mildness, and gentleness; as Christians, we are to show each other mercy and forgive one another. It was also part of the Roman Way. We see this with Pontius Pilate's effort to free Jesus Christ. However, this is not a demonstration by the Jewish leaders who desire Christ's death.

Dignitas - Dignity is a sense of self-worth, and personal pride, something that is lost today in our society, where so many seek to live off others' work. In 1 Peter 2:17, we read, "Treat everyone you meet with dignity. Love your spiritual family. Revere God. Respect the government."

Firmitas - Tenacity, Strength of mind, the ability to stick to one's purpose. Jesus tells us to stand fast to the very end. We, as Christians, are to be strong. The Romans shared this belief.

Frugalitas - Frugalness, economy, and simplicity of style, without being miserly. In John 6:12, we read, "When they were filled, He said to His disciples, 'Gather up the leftover fragments so that nothing will be lost.'" Today, how often do we see pastors seeking wealth, and it never seems to be enough? I recall the song "Would Jesus Wear a Rolex?"

Gravitas - Gravity; a sense of the importance of the matter at hand, responsibility, and earnestness, taking responsibility for the things we do and getting the jobs done. Congress here in America could learn something from this.

Veritas - Truthfulness, Honesty, speaking the truth is something that many fail to do, even the political and the media. Honesty to the Romans is also respectability to be correct. The image that one presents as a respectable member of society. The Bible teaches us not to bear false witness. Our media creates fake news, which is a lie to destroy the character of those who do not share their agenda.

Humanitas - Humanity: a manner of refinement, civilization, learning, and being cultured. Jesus said, "Blessed are the humble."

Industria - Industriousness: A Roman was to be hard working to provide for oneself. Paul, in his letters, often spoke of how he earned his way. It is because Paul was not only a Jew but a Roman citizen. Today, we have millions of people who wish to be taken care of like one's pet. They want to live off of the work of others.

Pietas - Dutifulness; is more than religious piety; respect for the natural order socially, politically, and religiously. It includes the ideas of patriotism and devotion to others. But, unfortunately, today, our leaders are more concerned about themselves, while many people show no sign of patriotism.

Prudentia - Prudence the ability to be foresight, have wisdom, and personal discretion. "I, wisdom, dwell with prudence, And I find knowledge and discretion." (Proverbs 8:12 NIV)

Salubritas - Wholesomeness; to be healthy and clean. The Romans had hot water for bathing.

Severitas - Sternness; is to perform gravity, self-control, something that those out of the seven churches in Turkey did not demonstrate.

Viewing this list of characteristics, we see that many are within the Bible and Christ's teaching. Living to a higher standard was already part of the Roman culture. Now, accepting Jesus Christ would make them acceptable in the Eyes of God and make achieving these qualities more accessible through the Holy Spirit's power. The Roman culture was prime for accepting Christ.

Public virtues:

Besides personal private virtues aspired by individuals, Roman culture also strove to uphold virtues shared by all of society in common. Note some of the attributes individuals aspire to are also public virtues. The community as a whole seeks them. The Romans shared these virtues by minting them on coinage; in this way, they shared their message with the classical world. In many cases, these attributes personified their deities as a way of showcasing virtue.

Abundantia - Abundance, Plenty; is the idea of enough food and prosperity for all society segments.

Aequitas - Equity is fair dealings both within government and among the people. It would require the virtues to be exercised by individuals in power and with each other. It is an idea of how God would want his people to govern and treat each other. Here is an area we do not see our leaders performing today. Also, they were not practiced in the Jewish communities that believed that Gentiles were an inferior race. Jews and Muslims still hold this view that those who do not share their belief are inferior. The Jews refer to the Gentiles as the Goyim and the Muslims as the Infidels; both have a negative connotation. You only need to read their sacred books to know this is accurate and truthful.

There is no doubt that history shows Roman Leaders who were evil. However, what is present here are the beliefs held by the people of Rome, something that is seldom or never mentioned.

Bonus Eventus - Good fortune is the hope for positive events.

Clementia - Clemency was a sign of mercy shown to other nations.

Concordia: Concord is harmony among the Roman people and also between Rome and other nations. Also, something that individuals were to share.

Felicitous - Happiness is a personal and nationwide celebration of the best aspects of Roman society.

Fides: Confidence; for the Romans, this is good faith in all commercial and governmental dealings. For the

Christian, it is confidence in God and honest business deals.

Fortuna - Fortune, for the Romans, is an acknowledgment of positive events not far from the gift of God's blessing.

Hilaritas - Mirth, rejoicing, An expression of happy times; the Roman Christians found this to be part of what they ready did.

Lustitia - sensible laws and governance express justice. But, unfortunately, it seems today that those in government have a different set of rules.

Laetitia - Joy, Gladness is the celebration of Thanksgiving, often of the resolution of a crisis.

Libertas - Freedom is a virtue that has been subsequently aspired to by all cultures. The forefathers of the USA understood the importance of freedom.

Nobilitas - Nobility; Noble is an action within the public sphere.

Ops - Wealth is the acknowledgment of the prosperity of having more than one needs.

Patient - Endurance, Patience is the ability to weather storms and crises.

Pax - Peace is a celebration of peace among society and between nations. The most extended period in history with the most prolonged peace between nations was during the Roman Empire. No other country during any period in history can make that claim.

Pietas - Piety, Dutifulness, People are paying honor to the gods. We Christians are to pay homage to the Holy Trinity.

Providentia - Providence, Forethought, is Roman society's ability to survive trials and manifest a higher destiny. Here again, the Romans, before coming to Christ, understood the necessity of surviving trials.

Pudicita - Modesty, Chastity, is a public expression that belies the accusation of "moral corruptness" in ancient Rome. Instead, the Roman people practiced modesty.

Salus - Safety is a concern for public health and welfare. The Romans believed this to be necessary. So, the Romans built 5,000 miles of roads throughout the Empire and provided for the safety of travelers. They even offered brochures for the Inns along the streets.

Securitas - Confidence, Security brought by peace, and efficient governance that protects the nation's people.

Spes - Hope is the ability to hold on to good things, mainly during difficult times.

Uberitas - Fertility: The government's concern is mainly for agriculture.

Virtus - Courage is strength in the face of pain or grief, a quality mainly desired of leaders within society and government and of Christians to stand fast.
From this list, we can see that the Roman citizens already desired virtues for being a better individuals and a better citizen. Therefore many of these same characteristics were to be found in Christianity. It was not difficult for the Romans to accept them, along with Jesus Christ. Also, the Roman Christians experienced persecution for not being willing to worship Caesar as God. Caesar fed many Christians to the lions. It did not take place in the seven churches.

When we take a closer look at the seven churches, we don't find the same conditions; the communities are more diverse, and Satan's throne is there and his synagogue. The fact that the term synagogue can only imply a Jewish community practicing the Babylonian Talmud is present. The Roman pagans did not worship in a synagogue, nor did Catholics.

To conclude, perhaps Rome, like a few other cities with Christian communities, did not require a warning from Jesus Christ because they were far more faithful than these seven communities of believers. How many atheists, liberals, conservatives, and so-called Jews and Christians could live up to these standards? The Romans may not have had a religious code like the Torah-practicing Jews, but the one they had made it easy to accept Jesus.

We learn a great deal about Italians' nature from James Ernest Shaw in his book titled *'An Italian Journey.'* Shaw quotes many famous authors who have many claims about Italian' character and 'Dolce Vita.'

For example, E. M. Forster wrote, "Love and understand the Italians, for they are more marvelous than the land."

Here are several others: Samuel Johnson, an English essayist: "A man who has not been in Italy, is always conscious of an inferiority, from his not having seen what expectation a man should see."

D.H. Lawrence, English novelist: "And that is ... how they are. So terribly physically all over one another, they pour themselves one over the other like so much melted butter over parsnips. They catch each other under the chin, with a tender caress of the hand, and they smile with sunny melting tenderness into each other's face."

George Clooney, American actor: "I think people in Italy live their lives better than we do. It's an older country, and they've learned to celebrate dinner and lunch, whereas we eat as quickly as we can to get through it."

John Lydon, English lead singer of The Sex Pistols: "Move to Italy. I mean it: they know about living in debt; they don't care. I stayed out there for five months while I was making a film called 'Order Of Death,' and they've really got it sussed. Nice cars, sharp suits, great food, Stroll into work at 10, lunch from 12 till three, leave work at five. That's living!"

"I love places that have an incredible history. I love the Italian way of life. I love the food. I love the people. I love the attitudes of Italians." – Elton John.

"What is the fatal charm of Italy? What do we find there that can be found nowhere else? I believe it is a certain permission to be human, which other places, other countries, lost long ago." - Erica Jong, American novelist.

Shaw, in his book, mentions his desire to understand why Italians are so unique. Why, for example, do they use the same word for greeting and parting? The term Ciao is the shortened version of Il suo schiavo "I am your servant/slave." It later became Sciao, which became the present short, cheerful Ciao. It became a clue for Shaw into the Italians' nature, but not the actual understanding of their unique character. I ask you how many cultures greet each other with the notion that I am your servant and then perform as such. Shaw discovered on several occasions when he needed help how the Italians would go out of their way to assist him, to find a farm, a place to stay to sleep or eat.

After living on several farms for seven weeks, he returned home to Wisconsin. After nearly two years of reading and watching Italian films, he finally discovered the answer he sought in a film by Roberto Rossellini titled *Era Notte a Roma (American title - Escape by Night)*. Shaw notes in his book that the original movie opens with the following words.

On the 8th of September 1943, it was announced to the world that Italy had signed an armistice with the Allies. Who had landed in Sicily two months previously and who were now advancing up the peninsula toward Salerno.

After the 8th of September 1943, thousands, tens of thousands of allied prisoners, British for the most part, who had escaped from concentration camps, wandered through Italy seeking asylum for weeks and months from north to south, mingling with the Italia refugees, asking for hospitality in the countryside and the cities.

No one denied us hospitality. On the outside walls of the houses were hidden the posters containing the communities of the German High Command, threatening with death penalty for anyone giving asylum or aid to Allied military personnel.

Our lives were protected by the uniforms we wore. If we were caught, the worst that could happen to us was to be sent back to a concentration camp.

But for Italians who helped us, there was only one alternative firing squad.

In spite of this, no one ever denied us hospitality. None of these people ever acted for personal gain. Many were not even definitely on our side.
I believe that, for the most part, their actions were guided solely by a sense of Christian charity.

This revelation gives Shaw the answer to his question and why he wrote in his journal, *'Their hospitality feels completely natural.'*

Finally, J. E. Shaw realizes that graciousness and generosity are based on love and hospitality, as emphasized in the Bible. He states that every Catholic knows: *"Love the Lord your God with all your heart and with all your soul and with all your mind and with all your strength. The second is this. Love your neighbor as yourself."* Shaw concludes that the Italians took these commandments to heart and made them tradition so much that they were willing to die to live them. Every Italian act with the understanding: *"What you do for the least of these, you have to do for me."* (Matthew 25:40 NIV) However, the attitude goes beyond the point that the stranger could very well be Christ and how I treat him.

Jesus knew that the Roman, the Italian ancestor, would remember and make His two commandments of love, tradition, and way of life. Therefore, they did not require a warning as the seven churches in Turkey. Jesus knew that there was always a meal ready for Him should He arrive at their home!

Before we continue with Revelation, let us briefly look at some of the beliefs suggested by various groups within the Church as early as the fourth century, during Constantine's rule. The Church became divided on the nature of Jesus Christ. This division is still with us today. Some of the notions held by these groups were adopted by Islam, which claims that Jesus Christ is not the Son of God but a man; this belief begins with Arianism. The idea is that Jesus Christ is not equal to the Father by nature, but He is God's first creation. The founder of Arianism was Arius, who died in 336. Arianism asserts the belief that Jesus Christ is the Son of God who was begotten by God the Father at a point in time. Therefore, Arius claims that Jesus Christ has a beginning; this is a distinction between the Father and subordinate to the Father. Arius was a Christian presbyter in Alexandria, Egypt. Arius and his supporters were opposed to Homoousian Christians' theological views regarding the nature of the Trinity, a concept that Muslims reject today. The Arian idea of Christ believes that the Son of God did not always exist but was begotten by God.

Other forms of this view that disbelieve in the theology of the Trinity are. Docetists Gnostics claimed that the divine Jesus Christ would never stoop to touch flesh, which is evil. Jesus only seemed (dokeo, in Greek) human and just appeared to die, for God cannot die. They also suggest "Christ" left "Jesus" before the Crucifixion.

The Apollinarians believe that Jesus is not equally human and divine but one person with one nature. They stated that Jesus, in his human flesh, resided in a divine mind and will. He didn't have a human soul or spirit, and His divinity controlled or sanctified his humanity. The basis for this is John 1:14: "The Word became flesh," therefore not a human mind or will.

Modalists believe God's names (Father, Son, Holy Spirit) change with his roles or "modes of being" (like a chameleon). When God is the Son, He is not the Father. There is no permanent distinction between the three "persons" of the Trinity. Otherwise, you have three gods. "Hear, O Israel: The Lord our God, the Lord is one." (Deuteronomy 6:4 NIV) However, Jesus Christ stated, "The Father and I are one." (John 10:30 NIV)

Ebionites, a group of conservative Jewish Christians, claimed that God is one and understands Jesus by Old Testament categories. Jesus was merely a specially blessed prophet: 1 Tim. 2:5: "For there is one

God and one mediator between God and men, the man Jesus Christ."

Adoptionists did not deny that Jesus was unique, but they stated that at birth, not conception or baptism, God "adopted" the human Jesus. As a result, Jesus became God's unique Son, and God gave Him an extra measure of divine power, based on Luke 3:22, "You are my beloved Son, today I have begotten you."

However, this impact continues to this present day with such groups as the Jehovah's Witnesses and Islam's teachings. As a result of their convictions, these modern-day Arians produce many Biblical arguments to support their contention that Jesus is not God. Thus, though Arianism is false, Biblically, its doctrines force the Church throughout all generations to define what she believes regarding the person and nature of Christ. To conclude, those who hold to these views today are anti-Christ, someone who rejects Jesus Christ's true nature. If Jesus is not God in the flesh, then His sacrifice did not pay for sin. Now let us continue our journey through the Lord's account.

In September of 2003, Professor Dr. Frederick Zugibe of New York, Columbia University did not know that he was given a sample of Eucharistic from August 15, 1996, a consecrated Host for Communion from Buenos Aires, Brazil. Dr. Frederick stated that the sample you brought me is the heart muscle of the myocardium of the left ventricle. He continued to report that the patient had some form of thrombi; at certain moments, he could not breathe. He reported more about how this was proof that Jesus Christ is present in the Eucharistic and part of the Holy Trinity.

Throne in Heaven
Seven Seals

(4) "After this I looked, and behold, a door standing open in Heaven! And the first voice, which I had heard speaking to me like a trumpet, said, Come up here, and I will show you what must take place after this."

Let's repeat a line, "Come up here, and I will show you what must take place after this." What is about to take place will take place after John witnesses the opening of the seven seals! Let's continue with the next verse, back to the action.

2 "At once I was in the Spirit, and behold, a throne stood in heaven, with one seated on the throne. 3 And he who sat there had the appearance of jasper and carnelian, and around the throne was a rainbow that had the appearance of an emerald. 4 Around the throne were twenty-four thrones, and seated on the thrones were twenty-four elders, clothed in white garments, with golden crowns on their heads. 5 From the throne came flashes of lightning, and rumblings and peals of thunder, and before the throne were burning seven torches of fire, which are the seven

Spirit of God, 6 and before the throne, there was as it were a sea of glass, like crystal. And around the throne, on each side of the throne, are four living creatures, full of eyes in front and behind 7 the first living creature like a lion, the second living creature like an ox, the third living creature with the face of a man, and the fourth living creature like an eagle in flight. 8 And the four living creatures, each of them with six wings, are full of eyes all around and within, and day and night they never cease to say, 'Holy, holy, holy, is the Lord God Almighty, who was and is and is to come!'"

9 "And whenever the living creatures give glory and honor and thanks to him who is seated on the throne, who lives forever and ever, 10 the twenty-four elders fall down before him who is seated on the throne and worship Him who lives forever and ever. They cast their crowns before the throne, saying,"

11 "Worthy are you, our Lord and God, to receive glory and honor and power, for you created all things, and by your will they existed and were created."

This vision of Heaven is in John's present time, just as the church's condition was in his current time, with warnings of what could occur if conditions continued. This vision of Heaven is the very same today as it was then. The situation is better since Satan and his minions are no longer present. Things are about to get interesting. The 'Great Tribulation' is about to begin, not in some distant future, as some may think, but the very moment that John witnesses these events. The angel said, and I quote it again, "Come up here,

and I will show you what must take place after this."
Not in some future, but after he sees it.

The Scroll and the Lamb

(5) "Then I saw in the right hand of Him who was seated on the throne a scroll written within and on the back, sealed with seven seals. 2 And I saw a mighty angel proclaiming with a loud voice, "Who is worthy to open the scroll and break its seals?" 3 And no one in heaven or on earth or under the earth was able to open the scroll or to look into it, 4 and I began to weep loudly because no one was found worthy to open the scroll or to look into it. 5 And one of the elders said to me, "Weep no more; behold, the Lion of the tribe of Judah, the Root of David, has conquered, so that he can open the scroll with its seven seals."

In anticipation, we watch this scene can the Lion of Judah, the Root of David, opens the scroll with its seven seals. We also wonder what the scroll will reveal when opened. We are on the edge of our seats while we share John's vision. There is great anticipation to learn the contents of the scroll.

6 "And between the throne and the four living creatures and among the elders I saw a Lamb standing, as though it had been slain, with seven horns and with seven eyes, which are the seven spirits of God sent out into all the earth. 7 And he went and took the scroll from the right hand of him who was seated on the throne. 8 And when he had taken the scroll, the four living creatures and the twenty-four elders fell down before the Lamb, each holding a harp, and

golden bowls full of incense, which are the prayers of the saints. 9 And they sang a new song, saying, 'Worthy are you to take the scroll and to open its seals, for you were slain, and by your blood you ransomed people for God from every tribe and language and people and nation, 10 and you have made them a kingdom and priests to our God, and they shall reign on the earth.' 11 Then I looked, and I heard around the throne and the living creatures and the elders the voice of many angels, numbering myriads of myriads and thousands of thousands,12 saying with a loud voice."

"Worthy is the Lamb who was slain, to receive power and wealth and wisdom and might and honor and glory and blessing! 13 And I heard every creature in heaven and on earth and under the earth and in the sea, and all that is in them, saying, To him who sits on the throne and to the Lamb be blessing and honor and glory and might forever and ever! 14 And the four living creatures said, 'Amen!' and the elders fell down and worshiped."

First, we notice John is weeping because he first witnesses no one can come forward to take the scroll and remove the seals to open it. John witnesses Christ, who is the only one worthy of removing the seals due to his wounds, for being slain. In this dramatic scene, Christ comes forward with his bloodstained injuries as evidence that He is worthy of overcoming death. John is also witnessing those in Heaven proclaiming Christ as worthy.

This vision affirmed that only Jesus, the Son of God who died for man's sins and was resurrected from the dead, a victory over sin and death, is worthy to open the scroll. Since the dragon, the accuser has been cast out of Heaven with a third of the rebelling angels, we do not see or hear anyone claiming they are worthy, nor anyone claiming that Christ is not worthy. John also witnesses God handing Christ the scroll. One fascinating observation made by John is that Jesus Christ comes forward with a bloodstained wound

Before commenting on the bloodstained wounds, I would like to clarify one critical observation in this scene: the presence of both God sitting on a throne and Jesus standing before him. Here is where some people get confused or ask how can Jesus and God be one? After all, if God is sitting on a throne, and Jesus Christ is standing before God, it is clear that they are not the same being. Therefore, Jesus cannot be God since the Lord, our God, is One. (Deuteronomy 6:4) Hence, Jesus must be a specially created being and an adopted son. People have argued this point a thousand times or more for more than a thousand years. Jews and Muslims hold to this view today. However, here is what they fail to understand. God can do anything He wants. God can be omnipresent, or to put it in simpler terms, be in all places at one time. He can do that. We can't appear in two places at once with two different appearances using poly location. God can be in more than one place at a time in more than one form. He is God; He can do whatever He pleases.

We can also examine this characteristic by recalling, "God created mankind in his own image, in the image of God He created them; male and female He created them." (Genesis 1:27 NIV) A man has three bodies, mental, emotional, and physical bodies. These are minor types of God's Trinity. A result of being able to separate into three different forms with the use of poly location.

The problem with skeptics is they generate questions and theories based on mankind's ability. They fail to consider that God has capabilities far beyond human comprehension. If we keep that simple fact always in mind, then God is three different beings simultaneously, and with God, all things are possible.

Now, let us continue with John's witness of a Heaven event.

The Holy Spirit suggested in me that John here has observed a past event. We know in John 20: 16-20 he wrote this statement. "Jesus saith unto her, Mary, She turned herself, and saith unto him, Rabboni; which is to say, Master. Jesus saith unto her, 'Touch me not; for I am not yet ascended to my Father: but go to my brethren, and say unto them, I ascend unto my Father, and your Father; and to my God, and your God.' Mary Magdalene came and told the disciples that she had seen the Lord and that he had spoken these things unto her. 18 Mary Magdalene went to the disciples with the news: 'I have seen the Lord!' And she told them that he had said these things to her. 19 On the evening of that first day of the week, when the disciples were together, with the doors locked for fear of the Jewish leaders, Jesus came and stood among them and said, 'Peace be with you!' 20 After he said this, he showed them his hands and side. The disciples were overjoyed when they saw the Lord."

Keeping this idea in mind that Christ appears in Heaven with his fresh, blood-stained wounds, the 'Great Tribulation' timeline began with the resurrection. It is where things start to get thought-provoking and confusing at times to understand. Too often, these are future events. However, they are John's past, present, and future, while some of these events are also present in our history and future. There is no reason to think that Jesus Christ is in Heaven for two thousand years as a slain lamb before a call goes out for someone worthy to open the scroll and remove the seals. This event took place right after Christ's victory over sin and death.

In ancient times and the present, someone who is victorious, a winner, is given his trophy, prize, or crown right after the event, not years later. The fact that John witnesses the Heavenly host looking for someone worthy would indicate this event took place during John's lifetime and in his past. I will repeat it. "Come and see what will happen after this!"

There is also something fascinating going on here. In ancient times, a document to leave an inheritance (will) was often sealed as a sign of importance and legal documentation. So, we will have a scroll sealed with seven seals to show a sign of completion and significance. Interesting also that the only one truly worthy of opening a 'will' is the heir. Here, the question is first asked: who is worthy and the Lamb appears, and who is the Lamb but the Son of God who sacrificed his life to remove sin? Only the rightful heir can open the seals to a 'will.' Jesus is the Rightful Heir. He is also the obedient Son, one of the requirements of the 'will.' Only the obedient Son could inherit the provisions provided in the 'will.' What we have here is God's will written in a 'will.' We found today that a corporate seal is attached to some legal documents even today. Jesus Christ is also worthy because He is also the giver of the scroll, being part of the Trinity. "Then Jesus came to them and said, All authority in heaven and on earth has been given to me." (Matthew 28:18 NIV) Here, John witnesses the passing of authority to Jesus by handing Him the scroll.

There is another definition of the word 'seal,' a device or substance that joins two things together to prevent them from coming apart or to prevent anything from passing between them. The scroll is held together with seals so that it keeps something from happening. The removal of the seal permits something to be released. As in a 'will,' it allows the transfer of ownership. The removal of the seals passes legal authority to Jesus Christ; this further enrages Satan.

We are about to see not God's punishment but the release of the Dragon's insanity. The "will" provides the conditions and the clauses of the Kingdom that Christ has inherited. It explains, what is the present situation of the inheritance, and what is taking place. Jesus has inherited a Kingdom with problems. Each of the seven seals reveals the current state of His Kingdom. For example, your father dies, and in his will, he leaves you seven buildings. Each of the buildings has problems, needs repairs, bills need paying, and tenants owe rent. The government wants its taxes. You have to comply or lose the inheritance. Jesus Christ's Kingdom has Satan, and his demons are running wild and causing men and women to sin.

Well, this is the condition of Jesus Christ's Kingdom. There is also a clause in the will; God has a date when Jesus can return to take possession of His Kingdom. Jesus does not have the complete transfer of the inheritance until the completion of the will's conditions. The difference with this "Will" is that both Jesus and God have eternal life, so time is not an issue, or another way to express it is there is no particular deadline.

Therefore, God is still in control, and Christ cannot return and take full possession until God orders it by setting the date. Also, keep this Biblical fact in mind as we Journey through Revelation; "But do not forget this one thing, dear friends: With the Lord, a day is like a thousand years, and a thousand years are like a day" (2 Peter 3:8 NIV). Jesus Christ opened the scroll less than 48 hours ago by the spiritual clock of Heaven. Now, let's return to the scene in Heaven to observe what John is about to witness. When removing the seals, something is revealed and let loose.

The Seven Seals

Jesus is about to remove the seals on this scroll, and what they reveal is not God's wrath but the Dragon's madness. God is permitting these things to happen. The restraining rains vanish by removing each of the seals, just as God allows Satan to do something to Job. However, Satan has yet to learn that he still performs God's will because God uses Satan's insanity to punish those who follow Satan. Here, we can see why I placed Chapter 12 at the beginning of this discussion. Chapter 12 is a prelude to the condition of Christ's inheritance. Let's continue with John's vision.

(6) "Now I watched when the Lamb opened one of the seven seals, and I heard one of the four living creatures say with a voice like thunder, 'Come!' 2 And I looked, and behold a white horse! And its rider had a bow, and a crown was given to him, and he came out conquering, and to conquer."

We see he came out conquering and conquering. So in three thousand years, there were only 286 years of peace in the known world on the earth; this is not a collective number, but with the most significant amount of consecutive years of peace under Roman rule. Keep in mind that when John witnesses the seals being open, Vespasian, first as a Roman General, then as Emperor, and his son Titus destroyed Jerusalem and the Temple in 70 AD. Conquering was not something new; there had already been many conquerors. How many conquests have taken place since John wrote God's Revelation? Take a good look at history; this is not a new event that will take place in the future. It happened in our past, in our present, and it will happen in our future.

3 "When he opened the second seal, I heard the second living creature say, 'Come!' 4 And out came another horse, bright red. Its rider was permitted to take peace from the earth so that people should slay one another, and he was given a great sword."

Note: It is permitted God does not restrain Satan from killing. In the letters, we read Jesus telling the believers to remain firm to the end, which means some would die a martyr. Also, those non-believers would suffer as well. Islam kills over 100,000 Christians a year. The media, the voice of Satan, does not draw attention to this mass killing. The Armenian Holocaust was the Ottoman Islamic government's systematic extermination of 1.5 million Armenian Christians. One group of people has killed another over and over since the writing of this verse. Genrikn Yagoda, a Russian Jew, killed over 8 million Poles for Stalin between 1931-1933 before Hitler came to power. How many native Americans have died from genocide? I can go on and on with the mass killings right up to our present time.

5 "When he opened the third seal, I heard the third living creature say, 'Come!' And I looked, and behold, a black horse! And its rider had a pair of scales in his hand. 6 And I heard what seemed to be a voice in the midst of the four living creatures, saying, A quart of wheat for a denarius, and three quarts of barley for a denarius, and do not harm the oil and wine!"

As the rider moves, we see how often the earth's people undergo inflation and food shortages. There have been 141 famines since the writing of Revelation around the world. Today, we can look at nations in Africa and Venezuela that can't afford or even have food available. Yet, after all these famines, theologians want us to believe that these events have nothing to do with Revelation's prophecies.

7 "When he opened the fourth seal, I heard the voice of the fourth living creature say, 'Come!' 8 And I looked, and behold, a pale horse! Its rider's name was Death, and Hades followed him. And they were given authority over a fourth of the earth, to kill with sword

and with famine and with pestilence and by wild beasts of the earth."

Hades was the ancient Greek chthonic god of the underworld, which eventually took his name. In Greek mythology, Hades was the oldest son of Cronus and Rhea, although his father's last son regurgitated. With his brothers Zeus and Poseidon, Hades defeated their father's generation of gods, the Titans, and claimed rulership over the cosmos. The three brothers divided the treasure into three parts: Hades received the underworld, Zeus the sky, and Poseidon the sea. Therefore, Hades became the world underground, a place for the dead.

We also see that this rider is like the last two, but even killing with disease and famine. Our playbill adds information. History has recorded places in the past and present, and this continues today. The mosquito kills more people annually than man or any other creature. One example is the Antonine Plague, named after one of its possible victims, Marcus Aurelius Antoninus, the Emperor of Rome. The Roman historian named Dio Cassius records the plague. He wrote that 2,000 people were dying each day in Rome. That's roughly one-quarter of those who were infected during 165-180 AD, 65 years after John's death; as of this revision, nearly 2 million deaths worldwide due to COVID-19.

We need to keep in mind that these are not earthly riders but rather the action of the dragon's insanity. We already saw that the dragon desires to kill the spiritual offspring of the woman in Chapter 12. This vision was in John's lifetime. Therefore, these are revelations of things to come for his generation and beyond. Thus, much of this is in our past. If you disagree, I encourage you to use the Internet and research history to see just how often these things have occurred.

9 "When he opened the fifth seal, I saw under the altar the souls of those who had been slain for the Word of God and for the witness they had borne. 10 They cried out with a loud voice, 'O, Sovereign Lord, holy and true, how long before you will judge and avenge our blood on those who dwell on the earth?' 11 Then they were each given a white robe and told to rest a little longer until the number of their fellow servants and their brothers should be complete, who were to be killed as they themselves had been."

God and Christ do not kill believers; non-believers do, and they are Satan's followers, for they do his work. Think of all the innocent people who are being killed today because of their faith in Jesus Christ. Image how many have already died since Jesus Christ's crucifixion. John witnessed or heard many of his friends. The other apostles and disciples, those of his time and those of the future crying. "When will you judge and avenge our blood?" I often ask a similar question: When will you end all this evil, for I do not wish to see others tested? My body groans when hearing the killing of innocent people. No one should die in such a brutal manner.

John is the only Apostle who dies of old age. As I already mentioned, all of his fellow Apostles experienced a martyr's death. Many of the believers were tortured and killed. Some were fed to the lions or murdered by Jewish leaders and their followers, Zealots, or Roman rulers. Persecution began the day Christ was resurrected; this event started in John's past and is still going on today. By the time Christ ordered John to write, over sixty years of Christian persecution had already occurred, with many believers tortured and killed.

12 "When he opened the sixth seal, I looked, and behold, there was a great earthquake, and the sun became black as sackcloth, the full moon became like blood, 13 and the stars of the sky fell to the earth as the fig tree sheds its winter fruit when shaken by a gale. 14 The sky vanished like a scroll that is being rolled up, and every mountain and island was removed from its place. 15 Then the kings of the earth and the great ones and the generals and the rich and the powerful, and everyone, slave and free, hid in the caves and among the rocks of the mountains, 16 calling to the mountains and rocks, 'Fall on us and hide us from the face of him who is seated on the throne, and from the wrath of the Lamb, 17 for the great day of their wrath has come, and who can stand?'"

In May 526 AD, an earthquake struck Antioch's city, which was then part of the Byzantine Empire, the Eastern form of the Roman Empire. The death toll was over 250,000. The quake also caused Seleucia Pieria's port to rise by nearly one meter, produced in the silting of the harbor. The ruins of this ancient city lie near the modern city of Antakya, Turkey.

Another event killed many immoral people, but it occurred in 79 AD, eleven years earlier than most theologians claim that John wrote Revelation. However, if Christ opened the seals when his wounds were still bloodstained, this event occurred after the seal's removal. It was the eruption of Mount Vesuvius, and John may have witnessed a past incident. Mount Vesuvius, a volcano near the Bay of Naples in Italy, is hundreds of thousands of years old and has erupted more than 50 times. Its most famous eruption is when the volcano buried the Roman Empire's ancient city of Pompeii. It left the town buried under ash for 17 hundred years. The dust "poured across the land" like a flood; one witness wrote and shrouded the city in "darkness...like the black of closed and unlighted rooms." Two thousand people died, and the town was abandoned for almost as many years. This event took place just nine years after Rome destroyed the Temple in Jerusalem. John died in 100AD, and some say he wrote Revelation in 90-95Ad, but is it possible that he knew of the event and later learned why it happened?

Here, we have our first look at a vision that causes questions. Did an event ever take place that would appear to satisfy the images here? The black sun and red moon with stars of the sky falling to the earth are possible during a solar eclipse, with comets flying by during an earthquake. Historians have recorded one such event during the crucifixion of Jesus Christ. Other such incidents have occurred. Some scientists believe that earthquakes are more likely to happen during a solar eclipse; this is also a natural catastrophe, which differs from manufactured ones.

(7) "And after these things I saw four angels standing on the four corners of the earth, holding the four

winds of the earth, that the wind should not blow on the earth, nor on the sea, nor on any tree."
2 "And I saw another angel ascending from the East, having the seal of the living God: and he cried with a loud voice to the four angels, to whom it was given to hurt the earth and the sea, 3 Saying, Hurt, not the earth, neither the sea nor the trees, till we have sealed the servants of our God in their foreheads."

Here is our first sign of our present or future. There is no way to research 12,000 from each tribe of Israel. A total of 144,000 have received the seal of God in their foreheads or other individuals as well. Notice the seal is not on their foreheads but in. It is essential because a mark on the forehead is an outward appearance, and we have already read from the seven churches that God and Christ disapproved of this external display. The mark on the forehead would represent one's belief and faith in God and Christ. This mark is in the form of one's fruit and faith. Since they are also to be virgins, it is also possible that they have already been collected and are standing ready with Christ. Since they are also virgins, the possibility is that they must be young, even pre-adolescent, for modern society has become very promiscuous.

9 "After this I beheld, and, lo, a great multitude, which no man could number, of all nations, and kindreds, and people, and tongues, stood before the throne, and before the Lamb, clothed with white robes, and palms in their hands;" 10 "And cried with a loud voice, saying, Salvation to our God which sits upon the throne, and unto the Lamb."

We watch John seeing a multitude of people from all nations, people, and tongues, and they are praising God and Christ for their salvation; these can only be believers. The 144,000 Israelis and the multitude must be believers in Christ who martyred since they already mentioned crying out under the altar. This scene is most likely of a future multitude in Heaven. These two groups arrive in Heaven only after their death since it would be people's souls over time. We have already read that John saw the martyrs under the altar after the fifth seal's opening. Therefore these two groups of believers have arrived after their death. There has been no mention of a harvest of living believers in Revelation so far. The rapture is a false doctrine created by John Darby in 1830; this is another example of misinterpretation. Non-Catholic Theologians believe that many will be taken to Heaven in a body like Enoch.

Some theologians accept Darby's notion based on Matthew 24:40, "Two men will be in the field; one will be taken and the other left." However, Darby and his followers fail to quote the verse before, which is, "And they were oblivious until the flood came and swept them all away. So will be the coming of the Son of Man." Jesus is saying the wicked had no clue until the flood water destroyed them. "The righteous perish, and no one takes it to heart; the devout are taken away, and no one understands that the righteous are taken away to be spared from evil." (Isaiah 57:1)

When you read Matthew Chapter 24, you get a slightly different message than Darby's Jesus answered: "Watch out that no one deceives you. 5 For many will come in my name, claiming, 'I am the Messiah,' and will deceive many. 6 You will hear of wars and rumors of wars, but see to it that you are not alarmed. Such things must happen, but the end is still to come. 7 Nation will rise against nation and kingdom against kingdom. There will be famines and earthquakes in various places. 8 All these are the beginning of birth pains."

9 "Then you will be handed over to be persecuted and put to death, and you will be hated by all nations because of me. 10 At that time many will turn away from the faith and will betray and hate each other, 11 and many false prophets will appear and deceive many people. 12 Because of the increase of wickedness, the love of most will grow cold, 13 but the one who stands firm to the end will be saved. 14 And this gospel of the kingdom will be preached in the whole world as a testimony to all nations, and then the end will come."

It does not seem Jesus is saying, don't worry, I will rapture you before these terrible things happen. When we consider the verse before Matthew 24:40, it is clear the reference is that Jesus is speaking of the wicked will die, not a rapture to Heaven in a living body. Also, keep in mind Noah and his family were left behind on an Ark. Jesus, in the letters to the seven churches, tells us to hold fast to the end. Hence, we have yet to read any remark thus far that would indict a rapture of believers. Notice the words 'the righteous perish, and no one takes it to heart,' again, the meaning is exact: they die.

Seven Angels with Trumpets

Seventh Seal and the Golden Censer

(8) "When he opened the seventh seal, there was silence in heaven for about half an hour. 2 And I saw the seven angels who stand before God, and seven trumpets were given to them. 3 Another angel, who had a Golden Censer, came and stood at the altar. He was given much incense to offer, with the prayers of all God's people, on the golden altar in front of the throne. 4 The smoke of the incense, together with the prayers of God's people, went up before God from the angel's hand. 5 Then the angel took the censer, filled it with fire from the altar, and hurled it on the earth; and there came peals of thunder, rumblings, flashes of lightning and an earthquake."

People, on some occasions, have witnessed what science calls earthquake-lights. Therefore, it is safe to say that this incident has more than likely taken place in our past. The number of earthquakes has increased. We have the Crete Earthquake and Alexandria Tsunami in Greece and Africa on July 21, 365 AD. Thus, we have an example of a significant event;

there were more than likely many less violent earthquakes resulting from the Golden Censer's pouring during the past 19 hundred years.

There are 30 minutes of silence in Heaven before the Seven Angels with Trumpets appear. It is equal to nearly 21 years of Earth time; based on 2 Peter 3:8, "One day is like a thousand years," or an hour is almost 42 years. It is a period of quiet before the storm. It is also a brief rest between one day to the next. In Genesis, we know that God marks each day, and it says, "God saw all that he had made, and it was very good. And there was evening, and there was morning, the first day" (Genesis 1: 31). There is this hint of a pause where God looks at what He did before He begins to create the next day. We have another indication of a break: God leaves Adam and Eve alone in the garden. "Then the man and his wife heard the sound of the Lord God as he was walking in the garden." (Genesis 3:8). This pause seems to be that moment when God evaluates what has taken place before making His next move.

I remember how my father would stand quietly for a half-hour or more just looking at the job he had just completed. He was judging how it turned out. Often I find myself doing the very same thing. Based on the evidence in Genesis, I believe that God takes a moment to assess what he has done or what others have done. We will see that this event seems to mark the ending of a series of events, "And there came peals of thunder, rumblings, flashes of lightning and an earthquake."

Seven Angels with Trumpets

Seven Angels with the Seven Trumpets are now entering the stage; this is where we, in our reading, find many theologians missing the point or are just skipping over it. We have read through the first seven chapters of Revelation, and it is clear that many events have already taken place more than once. Also, we see that the earlier Christians believed that Christ was to return during their generation from Paul's writings and others. Therefore the Great Tribulation would have also been a part of their age. We have read several times Christ having John write to the churches to hold fast to the end. This holding fast to the end means to the end of one's life, never giving up faith regardless of our surroundings and trials. Many of the tests were the result of Satan's doing. The natural events would be God's attempt to give humanity a chance to repent.

I wish to close here by restating this comment before moving on to the Trumpets. The removal of the seals revealed those items. It is the present condition of Christ's Kingdom during John's lifetime. The signs of what Satan is doing. The enemy is making his move on the battlefield. He lost the battle in Heaven, and now he wages war on earth against the children of the woman, the followers of the testimony of her Son Christ.

The Seven Angels lined up on center stage and are about to blow their trumpets, and what significance does that have? When in battle, the trumpeter would blow the charge as a sign to begin to do battle. Remember, there were no two-way radios in John's time, a more modern device, a cell phone, so a trumpet is a communication device. Joshua 6:3-5 (NIV), "March around the city once with all the armed men, do this for six days. Have seven priests carry seven trumpets of ram's horns in front of the ark. Then, on the seventh day, march around the city seven times while the priests blow the trumpets. When you hear them sound a long blast on the trumpets, have the whole army give a loud shout; then the wall of the city will collapse, and the army will go up, everyone straight in." Notice six days before the actual attack with all seven horns sounding together.

In Revelation, six trumpets sound as a warning before the final sounds enter the period of God's wrath. The seven angels are about to set in Christ's attack on his enemy, with the seventh trumpet sounding. These are events to have people repent before the final judgment, after which there is no opportunity for repentance. God provides these events in each generation for repentance, a sign of His Mercy.

Since the original writing of the commentary, a notion or idea came to mind that the Trumpets' sounding or perhaps one or more may occur on the Feast of Trumpets. The reason for this is that Jesus, the sacrificial Lamb, is sacrificed at the Feast of Passover.

6 "Then the seven angels who had the seven trumpets prepared to sound them. 7 The first angel sounded his trumpet, and there came hail and fire mixed with blood, and it was hurled down on the earth. A third of the earth was burned up, a third of the trees were burned up, and all the green grass was burned up."

An event occurred in Russia on June 30, 1908. An explosion over the sparsely populated Eastern Siberian Taiga flattened 770 sq. mi of forest with no known human casualties. The blast, a mid-air disruption, is classified as an impact event even though the object disintegrated at an altitude of 3 to 6 miles rather than hitting the surface of the Earth. The Tunguska Event seems to match John's description of a ball of blood red on fire falling to Earth, taking out trees, and no human life. Based on the size of the area, a minimum of 80 million trees were destroyed. The majority of trees grow in Russia, Canada, the United States, and China. In the southern hemisphere, it would be Brazil and the Democratic Republic of the Congo. In conclusion, this event could very well have been the result of the first Trumpet sound.

What is interesting about this date is that it is Rosh Chodesh. It is the name for the first day of every month in the Hebrew calendar, marked by the moon's birth; it is considered a minor holiday, akin to the intermediate days of Passover and Sukkot. "And on your joyous occasions, your fixed festivals and new moon days, you shall sound the trumpets over your burnt offerings and your sacrifices of well-being." (Numbers 10:10) The Tunguska event occurred on a day when the Jewish people were required to sound a trumpet.

8 "The second angel sounded his trumpet, and something like a huge mountain, all ablaze, was thrown into the sea. A third of the sea turned into blood, 9 a third of the living creatures in the sea died, and a third of the ships were destroyed."

We turn to our playbill and read after some research and discover several possibilities. The first is in an area part of three ancient kingdoms, Persia, Greece, and Rome. The first volcano is Akyarlar, belonging to the active Cos volcanic complex, Turkey's western volcanoes. Akyarlar is located south of the Seven Churches on the shore of the Aegean Sea. Presently, there is also the danger of 14 volcanos erupting in Turkey caused by the Turkish Plate's movement. Akyarlar may slide under the Euro plate, thereby causing Akyarlar to slip into the sea.

While I was writing yesterday, August 25, 2016, an earthquake took place in Italy due to Euro African plates moving toward each other. It could be the same movement that would cause Akyarlar to slide into the sea. There are present reports concerning Turkey. Imagine what would happen if 14 volcanoes were to erupt simultaneously; this is a possibility. It could cause the Rock of the Dome, built on the Temple's foundation, to collapse. And to open the way for the construction of the Third Temple.

Another possible mountain ablaze sliding into the sea is the Cumbre Vieja volcano on La Palma's island in the Canary Islands. The Canary Islands were part of the Roman Empire. Cumbre Vieja sliding into the ocean would generate a mega-tsunami. That would initially be about 1,000 meters high and would still be about 50 meters or roughly 150 feet tall when it reaches the US's eastern seaboard; this would look like a 15-story building moving toward the coast. A mega-tsunami could quickly take out ships in the Atlantic Ocean.

Finally, but not part of Daniel's ancient world kingdoms, is the Kilauea volcano in Hawaii, one of the most active volcanos in the world. Some people already believe that it will slide into the ocean. We can see that God works in an orderly fashion, one major event at a time. The very first chapter of Genesis would illustrate that clearly for us. The problem with these two volcanos is they are out of God's narrative setting.

There is also the possibility that John saw a dangerous asteroid the size of a mountain on fire, hitting the Earth. It would contaminate the ocean, thereby killing sea life and causing a massive tsunami, which would destroy ships; this is a possible scenario since the United States Government has been building underground cities. It would seem for the rich and powerful to escape from either nuclear war or natural catastrophes, such as meteors or asteroids, while the rest of the citizens die unknowingly, as in the days of Noah. "People will flee to caves in the rocks and holes in the ground from the fearful presence of the Lord and the splendor of His majesty when He arises to shake the earth." (Isaiah 2:19, NIV) Also, the scripture says, "Then the kings of the earth, the princes, the generals, the rich, the mighty, and everyone else, both slave and free, hid in caves and among the rocks of the mountains." (Revelation 6:15)

Common sense would suggest that only the wealthy and government officials could build an underground city to protect themselves from radioactive fallout. It doesn't take much to guess that the President and his staff and other government officials would have a safe place to hide while the rest of humanity dies in a sea of radiation.

Lately, there has the talk of a planet coming into our solar system named Nibiru; this could cause a significant change in gravitational pulls in our solar system and Earth. Meteors or an Asteroid that would pass could now hit us and possibly cause earthquakes, causing these first two events and the next two. However, as of July 15, 2019, nothing hypothesized has occurred. (I updated this date.) Let's get back to John and the next angel.

10 "The third angel sounded his trumpet, and a great star, blazing like a torch, fell from the sky on a third of the rivers and on the springs of water 11 The name of the star is Wormwood. A third of the waters turned bitter, and many people died from the waters that had become bitter."

Here, we need to sit back for a moment and wonder how the Lord has John see a third of the rivers and springs polluted by this one falling star. Since we have this imposing star falling from the sky after the third trumpet's sound, it lends one to think that it can't be a meteor or an asteroid because a third of the rivers and springs are not in one location. I decided to research this further. I discovered that the same five nations with the highest number of trees also have the most substantial freshwater order in Brazil, Russia, the United States, Canada, and China. A giant meteor or asteroid could quickly take out a third of the freshwater supply. It would even have radioactive material, which causes people to die, but an asteroid would need to be very large, and it would do much more damage than pollute the freshwater.

However, if John saw only three rivers, the Tigris, Euphrates, and the Jordan River, Wormwood, an asteroid, falling on just one river would be a third. Since John sees these things from the spirit world of Heaven, he only sees the rivers and springs, and the star is not an asteroid but an angel, just like the sun/angel that opens the abyss and sets Abaddon free. We will read about that in a later chapter. It also agrees with the location being with the setting of God's Drama.

"He turned rivers into a desert, flowing springs into thirsty ground." (Psalm 107:33). We already read, "The mystery of the seven stars that you saw in my right hand and of the seven golden lamp-stands is this: The seven stars are the angels of the seven churches, and the seven lamp-stands are the seven churches." (Revelation 1:20) Hence, Wormwood may be an angel who could sweep across the earth and touch and pollute a third of the rivers and springs. Finally, the vision is just a symbolic picture of God's Word, causing the waters to become bitter. We see that God has ordered angels to perform specific functions through the vision that John witnesses.

The difficulty in understanding this is a result of first trying to see it from a physical perceptive. It seems that many of the theologians undertake the task of interpreting what John observes into tangible realities, but John is viewing these from the point of Heaven's existence. Thus, we may imagine it to be some form of symbolism when, in fact, it is a spiritual reality when the reality is to be able to see it from how it looks from the spiritual realm. Hence, the angel touches the source of a third of the rivers and springs, and they become polluted, which is a very plausible explanation. When we consider that angels perform God's orders, it becomes clear that an angel can accomplish this task. "For he will command his angels concerning you to guard you in all your ways." (Psalm 91:11). God can also order them to destroy the wicked. Let's continue viewing the drama.

12 "The fourth angel sounded his trumpet, and a third of the sun was struck, a third of the moon, and a third of the stars so that a third of them turned dark. A third of the day was without light, and also a third of the night."

Well, this is an event that has yet to happen. After all, we are still living with a 24-hour day. One should note that God created the sun and the moon to light the earth on the fourth day, and here, He is reducing the light at the sound of the fourth trumpet. Keep in mind that if the third of the day is without light, then it becomes night. Thus, we have a more extended period of darkness, much like Alaska during the fall-winter season, perhaps something else. However, are the sun, moon, and stars reduced in size? Therefore, what happens? Do they become smaller, or is the 24-hour day affected? If the sun was to begin smaller, the earth would enter into an ice age and there is nothing here that would suggest it. Let's examine a 16-hour day.

The curtain closes for a brief intermission as we take a moment to ponder this event. As I was writing this and producing my videos for YouTube, it puzzled me at first. It gave me some difficulty in understanding what could be possible for this to happen, shortening the day by a third. The idea was that the earth would need to increase its rotational speed to shorten the day. This prompted me to conduct some research. During the search, I found information produced by NASA describing a possible solution to reducing a third of the day's light. Verse 12 describes this as a natural phenomenon, which will reduce what constitutes a day (24 hours) by one-third to 16 hours. Isaac Newton's laws of motion can explain how specific quantities are related to the earth's rotational speed that provides for the length of a day and the exact position of the North Pole points called polar motion, or earth's wobble.

To understand the angular momentum theory, visualize the Earth spinning in space and on a tilted axis. It creates a downward motion, giving the earth momentum like that of a roller-coaster moving downward, gaining speed to move once again upward and down back. The Earth has an overall mass and rotation and, therefore, contains a specific amount of angular momentum. A change in force acting at a distance or closer to the Earth's rotational axis occurs, referred to as torque, and produces a change in inertia, especially near mountains. It alters a difference in the rate of the Earth's rotation.

An example of this principle occurs when skaters pull their arms inward during a spin. It changes the mass distribution to one nearer the center of the body. As a result, the rotation axis reduces the "moment of inertia," and the skater speeds up their spin because at that moment of inertia goes down, the spin rate must increase to retain the system's total angular momentum unchanged. If you need more proof, physics can provide the mathematical formula that reducing inertia will increase speed. If this occurs, the earth's shape may change to a much smaller sphere. As a result, the landmasses would come closer together and reduce the size of the oceans.

With Nibiru near our solar system, another fact in the formula could be the increase in torque; this would increase the speed of the earth's rotation, causing a 16-hour day, as prophesied in Revelation. As this planet draws closer to us, it seems a different phenomenon occurs. The question becomes how close it needs to be and when. Therefore, for the day to decrease by a third, the previous events introduced, the trumpets' sounding must take place in their proper order. If planet Nibiru, aka Planet X, is God's instrument, it would appear that the rotation increase due to a reduction in inertia and an increase in torque due to additional gravitational pull would accelerate the rotation. However, as of the editing of this writing, this phenomenon has yet to occur. Some would believe that nuclear warfare could cause this effect by reducing the sun, moon, and stars; this would be an artificial event. I think this will be God's work. Lastly, the passing of Nibiru has kept the amount of sunlight the same.

It also confirms that God has a specific plan that follows chronologically. It affirms that a random creation out of chaos is false. Earthquakes reducing the height of mountains and declining trees would bring the rotational axis closure to the center and minimize inertia. Gradational pull from an outside source increases torque and speed. So we must remember about global warming and concentrate on growing more trees with lots of prayers for repentance.

These were theories based on human science. However, in the spirit world, God could have an angle give the earth a sudden push and the planet to go faster, just as an angel polluted the rivers and springs, or God could order it so; this is only one possibility. We will know for sure once the event takes place. One more idea is that if God reduces the sun's size to produce less light, we will enter an ice age. However, John needs to see and write about a possible ice age.

Bill Gates introduced an idea to reduce the effects of what he believes to be the greenhouse effect by placing reflectors in the atmosphere to reflect a part of the sunlight, reducing the sunlight by a third. It would seem possible. Intermission is over; we have examined the first four trumpets, and only one has sounded. We return to our seats to see John witnessing an eagle flying, and John continues to speak.

A final possibility is from Fatima, Portugal, called the Miracle of the Sun, on October 13, 1917. A crowd of about 17 thousand people witnessed the sun move around in the sky. It had been raining, and they were all wet. However, when the sun returned to its place, the clothing on everyone was dry. Therefore, the final possibility is that God will order the sun to reduce in size.

13 "As I watched, I heard an eagle flying in midair call out in a loud voice: 'Woe! Woe! Woe to the inhabitants of the earth because of the trumpet blasts about to be

sounded by the other three angels!'" The statement "Woe! Woe!" Woe means the punishment is about to take place.

The theatre stage and house lights fade to black. The audio comes on loud, and we hear a narrator speak from the Book of Enoch. He had recorded the woes in Chapters 95, 96, 97, and 98. The woes are the punishment inflicted upon the non-believers and the wicked of all types. Here are the Woes of Chapter 95: 5-8. "Woe to you who feed upon the glory of the corn, and drink the strength of the deepest spring, and in the pride of your power, tread down the humble." Here, we have a woe for the drunkenness of power to control people, men like George Soros, who desire to rule the world.

6. "Woe to you who drink water at pleasure; for suddenly shall you be recompensed, consumed, and withered, because you have forsaken the fountain of life," These are people who are consumed with lust of the flesh.

7. "Woe to you who act iniquitously, fraudulently, and blasphemously; there shall be a remembrance against you for evil." We see plenty of people today who are grossly unfair and morally wrong, spreading lies and deception, fake news.

8. "Woe to you, ye powerful, who with power strike down righteousness; for the day of your destruction shall come; while at that very time, many and good days shall be the portion of the righteous, even at the period of your judgment."

Here are the Woes of Chapter 96, marked by verse.
6. "Woe unto you, sinners, who in the midst of the sea, and on dry land, are those against whom an evil record exists. Woe to you who squander silver and gold, not obtained in righteousness, and say, We are rich, possess wealth, and have acquired everything which we can desire." These are the thieves of the world!

20. "Woe to you, ye obdurate in heart, who commit a crime and feed on blood. Whence is it that you feed on good things, drink, and are satiated? Is it not because our Lord, the Most High, has abundantly supplied every good thing upon earth? To you, there shall not be peace," The murders and those who kill for pleasure.

21. "Woe to you who love the deeds of iniquity. Why do you not hope for that which is good? Know that you shall be given up into the hands of the righteous, who shall cut off your necks, slay you, and show you no compassion," Here we have those who enjoy evil deeds. We call these people sociopaths. They enjoy doing the work of Satan.

22 "Woe to you who rejoice in the trouble of the righteous; for a grave shall not be dug for you," We see this when people are happy at the persecution of Christians. They find pleasure in watching Christians suffer.

23. "Woe to you who frustrate the word of the righteous; for to you, there shall be no hope of life," Here are those who mock and insult Christians. They are those who cause righteous troubles.

24. "Woe to you who write down the word of falsehood, and the word of the wicked; for their falsehood, they record, that they may hear and not forget folly."

25. "To them, there shall be no peace, but they shall surely die suddenly," I find this to be suited for our media today. They prefer to create fake news, which is falsehoods and outright lying.

The Woes of Chapter 97:1-3 + 12-15, "Woe to them who act impiously, who laud and honor the word of falsehood. You have been lost in perdition and have never led a virtuous life." These are people without any respect for God, for themselves, or for others. Visit any major city, and you will find neighborhoods filled with the decay of all forms.

2. "Woe to you who change the words of integrity; they transgress against the everlasting decree," The deceivers that twist words to suit their needs. Again, these are members of the media and state and federal politicians who turn words like their father; the serpent did in the Garden of Eden.

3. "And cause the heads of those who are not sinners to be trodden down upon the earth. Woe to you who expand the crime of your neighbor; for in hell shall you be slain," People who lie against their neighbors falsely to the point where they accuse them of crimes they never commented. The Democrats and the media did this to President Trump, just one example.

12. "Woe to you who lay the foundation of sin and deceit, and who are bitter on earth; for on it shall you be consumed," These are those individuals that cause

others to sin. We find them in the movie and music industry mainly.

13. "Woe to you who build your houses by the labor of others, every part of which is constructed with brick, and with the stone of crime; I tell you, that you shall not obtain peace," This could apply to all those who live off of taxpayers, demand even more. Also, those who make a living from criminal activities by scamming people out of their wealth.

14. "Woe to you who despise the extent of the everlasting inheritance of your fathers, while your souls follow after idols; for to you, there shall be no tranquillity." These are people that are worshiping things and believe that they will find happiness in owning expensive items.

15. "Woe to them who commit iniquity, and give aid to blasphemy, who slay their neighbor until the day of the great judgment; for your glory shall fall; malevolence shall He put into your hearts, and the spirit of his wrath shall stir you up, that every one of you may perish by the sword." This woe is for those who kill and are executed by others who kill. Chicago has become an example of this with all the murders that occur there.

Finally, the Woes: Chapter 98:6-8, "Woe to you, ye sinners, when you shall be afflicted on account of the righteous in the day of the great trouble; shall be burnt in the fire; and be recompensed according to your deeds."

6. "Woe to you, ye perverted in heart, who are watchful to obtain an accurate knowledge of evil and to discover terrors. No one shall assist you," We are seeing Hollywood and DC sexual perverts and pedophiles coming to light.

7. "Woe to you, ye sinners; for with the words of your mouths, and with the work of your hands, have you acted impiously; in the flame of a blazing fire shall you be burnt," Enoch has the same conclusion for the wicked the lake of fire of Revelation.

8. "And now know ye, that the angels shall inquire into your conduct in heaven; of the sun, the moon, and the stars shall they inquire respecting your sins; for upon earth, you exercise jurisdiction over the righteous."

These were the woes in the Book of Enoch. Those before the flood and for those who face the final Day of Judgment. The next three trumpets are about to sound, bringing Woes to the sinful inhabitants of the earth. These wows are the pain of punishment for evil and wicked behavior. God will judge all on a final day by the same set of standards. Now begins the last three trumpets to sound as we watch them with John at the event. Lights come up on the stage, and we see the next angel. The last three trumpets are also the last chance to receive God's mercy.

(9) "The fifth angel sounded his trumpet, and I saw a star that had fallen from the sky to the earth. The star was given the key to the shaft of the Abyss. 2 When he opened the Abyss, smoke rose from it like the smoke from a gigantic furnace. The sun and sky were darkened by the smoke from the Abyss. 3 And out of

the smoke, locusts came down on the earth and were given power like that of scorpions of the earth. 4 They were told not to harm the grass of the earth or any plant or tree, but only those people who did not have the seal of God on their foreheads. 5 They were not allowed to kill them but only to torture them for five months. And the agony they suffered was like that of the sting of a scorpion when it strikes. 6 During those days, people will seek death but will not find it; they will long to die, but death will elude them."

Here is another example of the word star used for an angel. John sees an illumined figure falling to earth and refers to it as a star. The same idea occurs for the birth of Christ. "9 After they had heard the king, they went on their way, and the star they had seen when it rose went ahead of them until it stopped over the place where the child was. 10 When they saw the star, they were overjoyed. 11 On coming to the house, they saw the child with his mother, Mary, and they bowed down and worshiped him. Then they opened their treasures and presented him with gifts of gold, frankincense, and myrrh." (Matthew 2: 9-11 NIV) Notice that the star went on ahead of them. The magi perceived the illumination from our human experience of physical reality.

The fifth trumpet sounds and an angel falls from the sky, as did Satan; only this angel has a key to unleash a type of locust. The instinct is not to harm those who have the seal of God, which means the Holy Spirit's presence and covered with the blood of Christ. Now, we read a contrary view concerning the notion of rapture. Here is an appearance of people with the seal of God on their foreheads. It contradicts any idea of a rapture occurring before this event. There is a presence of those with the mark of God and Christ present. Therefore, they cannot be raptured. God punishes the non-believer but provides the believers as a witness because God desires that none should perish. (2 Peter 3:9) The recurring notion is that this resembles Exodus's event when the angel of death passed with blood over the door's mark.

When we look at the various chapters in both Leviticus and Numbers, we can read several events in which those who disobey God or even oppose Moses are punished or terminated. Here we have simple common sense those who are receiving torment and are suffering will witness those who are not. The hope is that they will ask and learn about salvation, but some may only harden their hearts and choose to harm those with salvation.

Again, to clarify the Book of Revelation, we go to our playbill to understand the woes' purpose. Enoch provides the answer to give a change of heart so sinners may ask for mercy and forgiveness. In Chapter 49, Enoch begins with verse 2: "In the day of trouble, evil shall be heaped up upon sinners, but the righteous shall triumph in the name of the Lord of Spirits. 3. Others shall be made to see that they must repent and forsake the works of their hands and that glory awaits them not in the presence of the Lord of Spirits, yet that by his name they may be saved. The Lord of Spirits will have compassion on them: for great is His mercy, and righteousness is in his judgment, and the presence of his glory, nor in his judgment shall iniquity stand. He who repents not before Him shall perish."

4. "Henceforward I will not have mercy on them, saith the Lord of Spirits," This passage from Enoch makes very clear God's purpose for the wows. Once the final woe is over, there will no longer be any opportunity for mercy and salvation.

The fifth angel has sounded his trumpet, the Abyss opens, and out of the smoke comes a plague, and John sees it as follows. 7 "The locusts looked like horses prepared for battle. On their heads, they wore something like crowns of gold, and their faces resembled human faces. 8 Their hair was like women's hair, and their teeth were like lions' teeth. 9 They had breastplates like breastplates of iron, and the sound of their wings was like the thundering of many horses and chariots rushing into battle. 10 They had tails with stingers, like scorpions, and in their tails, they had the power to torment people for five months. 11 They had as king over them the angel of the Abyss, whose name in Hebrew is Abaddon and in Greek is Apollyon (that is, Destroyer)."

John sees something that provides a means of gaining access to the Abyss and unlocks it. He then considers the imprisoned angel to come out with a fury, so much so that he manifests a black smoke as he climbs high in the sky. The smoke is a physical manifestation of his darkened spirit and the darkness that covered him and held him prisoner in the Abyss. It now causes darkness to block out the sun. His anger and hatred have created the locusts, and for this reason, he is their king, but God's Law of like-kind causes them to seek only evil those with an evil nature. And God said, "Let the land produce living creatures according to their kinds." (Genesis 1:24 NIV)

According to the Book of Enoch chapter 8, Azazel is one of the rebellious Watchers' leaders preceding the flood. He taught men the art of warfare, making swords, knives, shields, and coats of mail, and women the art of deception by ornamenting the body, dyeing the hair, and painting the face the eyebrows. He also revealed to man the secrets of witchcraft corrupted their manners, leading them to wickedness and impurity. Finally, God commands him to be bound hand and foot by the archangel Raphael and chained under the jagged rocks of Dudael, where he must abide in utter darkness until the great Day of Judgment, when God will cast him into the lake of fire.

We can safely suggest that while imprisoned, he created this army of insects. Imagine for a moment only one mosquito bite and how it itches. Now imagine your whole body covered with mosquito bites, driving you insane, day and night, for five months with no relief. Once again, we see how God will use evil to destroy itself. The Seal of God is the Blood of Christ that covers the portal of our soul. It is as if the Blood of a lamb covered a door and protected the Israelites. "They are to take some of the blood and smear it on the sides and top of the door-frames of the houses where they eat the animal." (Exodus 12:7). There are several additional provisions besides placing the Lamb's Blood around the door. There is also cooking of the Lamb and when and how eaten, and finally, burning the leftovers. Every detail of this action required one key ingredient, and it was faith. Israelites did it because they believed in God's Word that it would save them. Well, Jesus tells us that we must eat his flesh to have life within us. Jesus said to them, "Very truly I tell you, unless you eat the flesh of the

Son of Man and drink His blood, you have no life in you." (John 6:53 NIV) Today, we eat this form of manna as the symbol of the Lamb's body. This manna gives eternal life. The Blood covers the portal of our hearts, and His Body gives us eternal life. What causes Apollyon, the destroyer, King of the Locust, to Passover us is due to the Mark of Christ.

Just as in the first Passover, the blood over the door saved lives. Or was it their faith in the blood over the door that caused death to Passover? Jesus said to her, "Daughter, your faith has healed you. Go in peace and be freed from your suffering." (Mark 5:34 NIV). It is faith in the Holy Eucharist that gives us life. Those who did not have the blood over the door did not prepare the lamb, eat it, or burn the leftovers; their firstborn died. There is no magic in the blood of the lamb nor in eating it. The belief and obedience to God that Israel escaped death, so it is with the Eucharist. First Faith in Christ and obedience to his command.

There is one other element, and that is during the Mass, the bread offered is unleavened. It is similar to the unleavened bread provided with the Temple's blood sacrifice, the Bread of Presences, or the Showbread. "Fire came out from the presence of the Lord and consumed the burnt offering and the fat portions on the altar. And when all the people saw it, they shouted for joy and fell facedown." (Leviticus 9:24). During the Mass, the eternal sacrifice of Christ within the presence of the unleavened bread as in the Showbread. The priest asks that the Eucharist be acceptable, as is the offering in the Temple. We see how an earlier event foreshadows that later.

One should ask why this angel was imprisoned underground in the Dudael desert and where this desert is, in Gaza. In Enoch chapter 10, this is one of the angels of Genesis 6:2: "The sons of God saw that the daughters of humans were beautiful, and they married any of them they chose." In Enoch, Chapter 10 explains that Azazel left his position in Heaven to take a wife and have children; however, it was forbidden, for God had created angels with immortal life. Therefore, there is no need for them to have children. I will repeat, "God said to Raphael, Bind Azazel hand and foot; cast him into darkness; an opening in the desert which is in Dudael cast him in there. 7. Throw upon him hurled and pointed stones, covering him with darkness; 8. There shall he remain forever; cover his face, that he may not see the light. 9. And on the great day of judgment, let him be cast into the fire."

Dudael is located east of Jerusalem in the once Babylon territory and bears this fallen angel's name. In researching Dudael and the angel Azazel's location, I discovered first the place is just 15 miles east of Jerusalem in an area named after the significantly fallen angel. The site is called Aza by some or Gaza. Gaza/Aza was part of Israel long before Islam sprang into being. Archeologists have uncovered and documented the remains of a Roman-period synagogue in Gaza. The evidence is Judaic inscriptions on a column located today at the mosque of Gaza/Aza. The writing is a Hebrew-Greek inscription complete with Jewish motifs that mention Hananiah, the son of Jacob. Archeologists had dated it between the second or third centuries, four to five centuries before Mohammed lived.

The Ottoman 1839 census of Jerusalem demonstrated that Jews were still living in Gaza/Aza at the time. Therefore, it is evident by the historical and archaeological evidence that the Arabs/Muslims are invaders. They took the land by force through conquest and war. Azazel taught men the art of warfare and how to make swords, knives, shields, and coats of mail, for combat is one of Azazel's characteristics and that of his demon followers. It is here that the army of Abaddon's, aka Azazel locust, will come forth. Where else but a place believed to be the hole to the underworld? Where an angel is in prison for thousands of years and right where there is continuous killing, rape, and slavery is taking place, here in the land of Babylon, where the Euphrates will give birth to the woe.

The traits attributed to Azazel are war, violence, and terror. The Arabs/Muslims occupying Jewish Gaza/Aza, Syria, Jordan, Iran, and Iraq have perfected the homicide/genocide bombing, specifically targeting women, children, and the elderly to spread horror, fear, and death to destroy future generations of Jews and Christians. Azazel's demonic traits include a total disregard for life, even for their offspring. They have camps for young children to brainwash them into aspiring homicide/genocide bombers. Like ravening beasts, they will tear apart, from limb to limb, any Jew or Christian who ventures into their area, passing around the body parts and rejoicing in some form of Satanic ritual. They wish for the rest of us to believe they are a peaceful religion when demonstrating that they are nothing more than psychopaths using a belief system to justify their evil wickedness.

The other discovery was that they never mentioned Jewish rituals in the Christian world. Perhaps since there is no Jewish sacrifice taking place today, maybe even the Jewish community may have forgotten it. The Azazel Personification of Impurity Rite was not recognized as a deity, but as stated by Naḥmanides, a symbolic expression of the notion that the people's sins and their evil consequences were to return to the spirit of desolation and ruin, the source of all impurity. The very fact is that two goats are part of the ritual for atonement before God; one was sacrificed as an offering to God, and the other was sent into the wilderness to have the nation's sins depart.

On the one hand, the rite resembles the epha's sending off with the woman embodying wickedness in its midst to the land of Shinar in the vision of Zachariah (5: 6-11). On the other hand, letting the living bird loose into the open field in the leper's case, healed from the plague (Lev. 14:7). The people of Jerusalem viewed it as a means of ridding themselves of the sins of that year. The Babylonians or Alexandrians would pull the goat's hair to make it hasten forth, carrying the burden of sins away with it. (Epistle of Barnabas, vii.), "And the arrival of the shattered animal at the bottom of the valley of the rock of Bet Ḥadudo, twelve miles away from the city, was signalized by the waving of shawls to the people of Jerusalem, who celebrated the event with boisterous hilarity and amid dancing on the hills." It is here where we get the term scapegoat.

This rite also foreshadows the crucifixion. Jesus Christ and Jesus Barabbas stand with Pontius Pilate before a crowd to select which is to be sent free.

(Matt. 27:17). As in the Azazel Rite, one goat is a chosen offering to God, and the other to be sent away with their crimes. We have Christ, a Lamb without blemish to be crucified, and Barabbas, the criminal who is set free from his sin. Therefore, the rite of atonement would be complete. A fascinating side note is they are both named Yeshua or Jesus. Here we have Jesus the Anointed/Christ and Jesus, the Father/Bar Abbas' son. The two Jesus replace the symbols with the two goats that foreshadowed this event. One Jesus is the sacrifice, and the other Jesus is to be set free. We have here the fulfillment of the sanctified rite of Azazel.

Hence, we have this fallen angel from the abyss leading a charge of locusts on the inhabitants who have commented on the very acts of wickedness they sent his way. In conclusion, the Pharisees and the Sadducees unknowingly performed the rite just as the Lord ordered. They failed to understand that the risen Christ was a symbol that mercy, forgiveness, and the removal of sin had taken place once and for all. Also, atonement for sin annually by an animal, which did not remove sin, was no longer necessary.

One more playbill footnote: a plague of 1 million locusts swarmed into Southern Israel from Egypt on March 7, 2013, but it only attacked the crops as locusts do. However, the insect of Revelation is a new breed that will attack the non-believer in Christ. Do we need to ask ourselves why all this happens in the same area? Let's put aside our playbill and return to witness what is next on the stage and a more recent swarm on March 4, 2019; these are warnings.

12 "The first woe is past; two other woes are yet to come. 13 The sixth angel sounded his trumpet, and I heard a voice coming from the four horns of the golden altar that is before God. 14 It said to the sixth angel who had the trumpet, "Release the four angels who are bound at the great River Euphrates." 15 And the four angels who had been kept ready for this very hour and day and month and year were released to kill a third of mankind. 16 The number of the mounted troops was twice ten thousand times ten thousand. I heard their number."

The number would be 200 million, but not necessarily all men. We quickly glance back at the notes in our playbill for some background information on this second woe from the sixth trumpet. Here we have another new clue to add to this list of hints concerning the place, the beast, the false prophet, and the harlot. Seven Churches are in Western Turkey, one with the throne of Satan, false teaching from a Jezebel, a synagogue of Satan, lukewarm Christians, idolaters, and a volcano south of the churches and on the West coast of Turkey that may slide in the sea. It was once a part of Babylon, Persia, Greece, and Rome, with its second capital in Istanbul. The fallen angel Azazel/Abaddon is coming out of a hole in Gaza. We see that four angels go from the Euphrates River, which has its origin in Southern Turkey. We have yet to have one clue putting anything on Italy's peninsula, or even America as so would think, but many pointing to Turkey, part of Babylon. This area is also where many Jews and Israelites in the Diaspora lived.

Before we continue, a significant point needs clarification. It is a minor detail that most theologians always neglect to take into consideration or deliberately do so. That is Nebuchadnezzar's Kingdom's size and that his Kingdom will be replaced by others before the Kingdom of God replaces it. God has given Nebuchadnezzar a dream about his Kingdom, and God gave Daniel the interpretation of his dream. The problem becomes when Theologians unknowingly expand Nebuchadnezzar's Kingdom to include the Roman Empire's boundaries indirectly.

There is something else that needs consideration, and that is the value of Nebuchadnezzar's kingdom. The territory of Babylon becomes less influential, and its wealth lessens with each new conquer. God has shown Nebuchadnezzar that his kingdom will decay from the head down. When we view the Roman Empire's accomplishments, we find a network of over 50,000 miles of roads that would take you from any part of the Empire to the other, with brochures of inns along the way. The Romans developed the use of the arch. That gave them the ability to create more magnificent spaces and the use of round tops. The arch with a wedge stone provides for a more durable stone structure to handle the weight.

The Romans made many contributions to construction. They constructed numerous aqueducts to bring water from distant sources into cities and towns, supplying public baths producing hot water, restrooms, fountains, and private households. They developed the means to flow water upwards. At other sites, aqueducts also provided water for mining operations, milling, farms, and gardens. They were able to flood the coliseum to have a ship-sea battle for the audience. Another contribution to Roman Architecture is the indoor mall. The building, though the shops are gone, can still be viewed by tourists today. Rome today is called the "Eternal City" because we can see antiquity side by side with modern architecture.

Rome was a Republic with a senate and systems of governing that we use today. The list of Roman accomplishments is many. Therefore, though, in Nebuchadnezzar's Kingdom, the territory of Babylon no longer had its earlier wealth. Rome, however, was a wealthy nation.

When we consider Nebuchadnezzar's dream, we need to focus on the territory of his kingdom. God was showing him in a dream what would happen to his kingdom. Everything mentioned thus far in Revelation continues to deal with Nebuchadnezzar's Kingdom, which includes the territories of Israel, Turkey, Syria, Iran, and present-day Iraq. Nebuchadnezzar's kingdom did not have the lands of Greece and Rome. It is the setting for God's Drama.

Therefore it is false teaching to add anything beyond Babylon's borders. God the Author has provided the setting for His Drama of Darkness to Light. There is no rejection of Daniel's interpretation revealed by God. The focus is on Nebuchadnezzar's Kingdom and nothing else. It is part of the land that God gave to the people of Israel, the descendants of Shem, with many of the other nations, the descendants of Ham. All of the events recorded in the Bible prior to Christ's sacrifice, except for Egypt, occur in what was once Babylon.

What is also present is something not written. With each new occupation of Nebuchadnezzar's kingdom, his kingdom decays. Gold slowly, over time, becomes iron and, finally, clay. The empire falls from the glory of gold to clay until nothing is left. Theologians forget to mention that Nebuchadnezzar began idol worship shortly after Daniel interrupted his dream, thus starting his kingdom's fall. The very same thing occurs with Israel. We can read it many times throughout God's Drama. Israel witnessed the Power of God in Exodus, and the first chance they got, they built a Golden Calf.

Let's replay this scene in Revelation; we heard it said to the sixth angel who had the trumpet, "Release the four angels who are bound at the great River Euphrates. 17 The horses and riders I saw in my vision looked like this: Their breastplates were fiery red, dark blue, and yellow as sulfur. The heads of the horses resembled the heads of lions, and out of their mouths came fire, smoke, and sulfur. 18 A third of mankind was killed by the three plagues of fire, smoke, and sulfur that came out of their mouths. 19 The power of the horses was in their mouths and in their tails; for their tails were like snakes, having heads with which they inflict injury."

This description was a little tricky at first for several reasons. One is that a horse and rider was the symbol of the nation of Khazar, many Turkish people who occupied a large part of the southern, western area of Russia from the 6th to the 11th centuries and who converted to Judaism in the eighth century, referred to as Ashkenazi Jews. They are more likely to be fair-skinned, blue-eyed Jews of today. The breastplates also provided difficulty since the colors are red, dark blue, and yellow. These are the colors of gold, bdellium, and onyx, and people used to make breastplates. The mentioning of these stones occurs in Genesis 2:11-12 in the land of Havilah near Eden, which is part of today's Turkey.

I spent a week thinking and meditating on this event while sitting in my backyard, my solitude garden. It is a small, modest, peaceful monastery. Jesus would often go to a garden to pray. "Then Jesus went with his disciples to a place called Gethsemane, and he said to them, 'Sit here while I go over there and pray.'" (Matthew 26:36 NIV) We all need a place where we can reconnect with God through the Holy Spirit. The needs and concerns of the day, work, family, news, and problems can often disconnect us from the Lord. We need a place to recharge and focus on the Lord to help us get through the day. I found that I was under attack, not in the physical sense but in the spiritual sense. The attack was going through my conscious mind as a means to distract me from the writing. I would wait until the "Still Small Voice" of the Holy Spirit would give me a word of insight, "for the Holy Spirit will teach you at that time what you should say." (Luke 12:12). To get a clear understanding of what is the meaning of these symbols. What came to me was that the plagues would originate from the northern portion of the Euphrates. The Land of Southern Khazar, the land that was once Havilah, because of the stones'

Since it was a plague and not a war where soldiers die and kill, an epidemic causing death. I searched for pictures of insects to get a good look at them close up, and there were many nearly fitting the description. Also, the number of 200 million and the fact they came out of the Euphrates River made it more plausible that insects carry a new disease. The following picture and thought that came to mind were the insects could deliver venom from either a bite or a sting. Today, we have a new disease carried by mosquitos called Zika. Therefore, out of the Euphrates, we have insect-killing people with a plague. Who are the people who will die from this plague but those who worship a false god and deny Christ? When we examine the area, we have Islam killing Christians to eliminate them from the face of the earth. Therefore, we can safely assume that it will be Muslims who will die from this plague.

A second idea came to me that these are symbols of an unseen plague caused by toxic gas. Fire burning sulfur will create a poisonous gas. Three items are needed: sulfur, heat/fire, and air to produce the fourth toxic gas. In the area along the Euphrates, we can find brimstone, which is sulfur. These angels are a spirit behind each of the items needed. The symbol also provides the location of the brimstone at the northern end of the Euphrates. Their release from the river will be the spark that starts the fire. The problem with this theory would be it does not have the potential for the pain to continue for five months. Also, there is the question of how far this plague will travel from its center. If, however, the disease is contagious, those infected could spread the disease worldwide.

20 "The rest of mankind who were not killed by these plagues, still did not repent of the work of their hands;

they did not stop worshiping demons, and idols of gold, silver, bronze, stone, and wood—idols that cannot see or hear or walk. 21 Nor did they repent of their murders, their magic arts, their sexual immorality or their thefts."

These four angels will release this plague that comes out of the Euphrates River, killing the non-Christian believers who live there. They will feel their sting and die a painful death. It isn't difficult to see that this very same area was once known as Babylon. Today it is where the highest form of hatred towards Christians exists. Therefore, wouldn't this be the place where God and Christ would have the most severe form of punishment? As I have already stated, Islam kills thousands upon thousands of Christians each year. Many of these children and teenagers are Christians with DNA from the twelve tribes of Jacob. It is more than likely the source of the 144,000 virgins that march with Christ.

The Angel and the Little Scroll

The scene on the stage in God's Drama has changed. John is viewing an event somewhere else. The setting is on earth. The incident more likely took place during John's time on Earth and went entirely unnoticed by people living in the area. We know that angels are only visible if God opens our eyes to see them, "And Elisha prayed, 'Open his eyes, Lord, so that he may see.' Then the Lord opened the servant's eyes, and he looked and saw the hills full of horses and chariots of fire all around Elisha." (2 Kings 6:17 NIV)

(10) "Then I saw another mighty angel coming down from heaven. He was robbed in a cloud, with a rainbow above his head; his face was like the sun, and his legs were like fiery pillars. 2 He was holding a little scroll, which lay open in his hand. He planted his right foot on the sea and his left foot on the land, 3, and he gave a loud shout like the roar of a lion. When he shouted, the voices of the seven thunders spoke. 4 And when the seven thunders spoke, I was about to write; but I heard a voice from heaven say, "Seal up what the seven thunders have said and do not write it down."

Seven, once again, is the number of completions. Seven thunders spoke, which would indicate that seven things were said in a booming voice, louder than a trumpet blast. The thunder represents the voice of God. Psalm 18:13 says, "The Lord thundered from heaven; the voice of the Most High resounded." In Genesis 1:3, we read, "And God said," so here we have God spoke seven utterances, and John is told not to write them, but John and Heavenly Host had heard it. Here we have a mystery, seven secrets possibly that God keeps from man, and Satan is no longer in Heaven. What comes to mind is you don't let the enemy know what you are planning.

We can also take a logical guess as to where this angel is standing. Since John faces the angel, his right foot is on water, and his left is on land. Therefore, it would be to John's left the water and to the right the land. Since John is on the Island of Patmos, it would suggest that the angel has his right foot on the Aegean Sea, with his left foot on the West Coast of Turkey or one of the islands nearby. Another possibility is Israel and the Mediterranean Sea. I make this suggestion because everything up to now has been in the territory of ancient Babylon. Once again, it is the location of the Garden of Eden.

5 "Then the angel I had seen standing on the sea and on the land raised his right hand to heaven. 6 And he swore by him who lives forever and ever, who created the heavens and all that is in them, the earth and all that is in it, and the sea and all that is in it, and said, "There will be no more delay! 7 But in the days when the seventh angel is about to sound his trumpet, the

mystery of God will be accomplished, just as he announced to his servants the prophets."

8 "Then the voice that I had heard from heaven spoke to me once more: 'Go, take the scroll that lies open in the hand of the angel who is standing on the sea and on the land.' 9 So I went to the angel and asked him to give me the little scroll. He said to me, 'Take it and eat it. It will turn your stomach sour, but in your mouth, it will be as sweet as honey.' 10 I took the little scroll from the angel's hand and ate it. It tasted as sweet as honey in my mouth, but when I had eaten it, my stomach turned sour. 11 Then I was told, 'You must prophecies again about many peoples, nations, languages, and kings.'" John was released from Patmos, so for a little while, he did prophesy again.

We have just taken a fast ride with John through several different scenes on the earth to witness other fallen angels, and until this angel and the small scroll, the sound for us was deafening that we didn't hear what was said. However, in Enoch's book, the same thing happens when he speaks about the angels who left their posts as watchers and took their wives. It would seem that God has given the order, and the final episode of the saga has begun. The curtain closes on this scene and opens with the stage set for Jerusalem.

Before the curtain reopens, we continue our journey. Let us pause for a moment to reflect on where we are in God's Drama. We are where human history witnesses a sign that the sun, moon, and stars have been reduced by a third. We have yet to record a mountain on fire sliding into the sea and turning the ocean blood red. As of today, we have not witnessed nor heard of a third of the freshwater becoming poison. Finally, the two plagues, one coming out of the Abyss and the other from the Euphrates River, have not occurred. I bring these events to you, the reader's attention, once again so that you may discern from the many false teachings present today. God is a God of Order and not chaos. We see this in Genesis and here in Revelation: Seals, followed by Trumpets and Bowls. Those who mix these events or have Bowels before the Trumpets are false teachers.

Two Witnesses & Seventh Trumpet

The scene is in future Jerusalem, where the two witnesses have arrived on the scene. There is an order to God's Drama, so these two cannot appear unless six of the seven trumpets have sounded. They arrive before the seventh and final trumpet sounds.

(11) "I was given a reed like a measuring rod and was told, "Go and measure the temple of God and the altar, with its worshipers. 2 But exclude the outer court; do not measure it, because it has been given to the Gentiles. They will trample on the holy city for 42 months. 3 And I will appoint my two witnesses, and they will prophesies for 1,260 days, clothed in sackcloth." 4 They are "the two olive trees" and the two lampstands, and "they stand before the Lord of the earth." 5 If anyone tries to harm them, fire comes from their mouths and devours their enemies. This is how anyone who wants to harm them must die. 6 They have power to shut up the heavens so that it will not rain during the time they are prophesying; and they have power to turn the waters into blood and to strike the earth with every kind of plague as often as they want."

The two witnesses will be in Jerusalem for 42 months. They will prevent it from raining, so the question surfaces: will it not rain on the whole earth or just over Israel for three and a half years? They will have the power to shut up the heavens to prevent rain when they are prophesying. These witnesses can turn the waters into blood and strike the earth with every plague as often as they want since the same epidemics occurred in Egypt. It would be safe to say that the diseases and holding back of rain may occur only in Jerusalem or all of Israel as if it were only in Egypt at the time of the Exodus.

Moses, often with God's help, terminates those who oppose him in the Book of Numbers. Another interesting note is not to measure the outer court but exclude it, for it belongs to the Gentiles. We know a Mosque, the Rock of the Dome, was built not only on the exact location of the Second Temple but also on the Temple's very foundation. There are plans to rebuild the Third Temple next to the Mosque on the court of Gentiles.

7 "Now when they have finished their testimony, the beast that comes up from the Abyss, will attack them, and overpower and kill them. 8 Their bodies will lie in the public square of the great city—which is figuratively called Sodom and Egypt—where also their Lord was crucified. 9 For three and a half days some from every people, tribe, language and nation will gaze on their bodies and refuse them burial. 10 The inhabitants of the earth will gloat over them and will celebrate by sending each other gifts because these two prophets had tormented those who live on the earth."

As mentioned in the Book of Enoch, Abaddon, aka Azazel, who was released from the Abyss after the fifth trumpet sounded, is still accessible on the earth's surface. Here John writes, or someone uses the term beast instead of a fallen angel. The inference may be that Abandon behaves like a beast. At this point, I wondered how they would assassinate these two witnesses, then I remembered. "Then the Lord opened the eyes of Balaam, and he saw the angel of the Lord standing in the way with his drawn sword in his hand, and he bowed to the ground." (Number 22:31). God sent the angel to kill Balaam, so here we have a fallen angel who kills the two witnesses; this opens the door for how some people may die and why it is essential to pray for mercy, forgiveness, and protection.

Abaddon is not Satan the Dragon because he is the angel imprisoned in the Abyss, perhaps since Enoch's time before the flood. He is now free to kill the two witnesses before Raphael receives orders from God, "And in the great day of judgment let him be cast into the fire." (Enoch 10:9). Now Abaddon's time has run out, and his destiny is eternal suffering in the lake of fire.

While meditating on the character of Abaddon, aka Azazel, and the four angels imprisoned in the River Euphrates, I contemplated the notion of why the dragon wasn't in chains and imprisoned. The idea came to me first that he never left his station in Heaven. He is "the accuser of our brethren has been thrown down, he who accuses them before our God day and night." (Rev 12:10) He also causes a rebellion. Therefore, we can safely assume he causes it. By deceiving the others into falling and observing their imprisonment, he can also accuse God of tyranny to get them to rebel. The serpent indirectly does that too Eve. The serpent tempts, but he doesn't eat the fruit.

Richard Dawkins, the atheist, has voiced the very accusations referring to God, titled 'The God Delusion.' Dawkins may not realize that he is spewing Satan's words. Dawkins says: "The God of the Old Testament is arguably the most unpleasant character in all fiction: jealous and proud of it; a petty, unjust, unforgiving control-freak; a vindictive, bloodthirsty ethnic cleanser; a misogynistic, homophobic, racist, infanticidal, genocidal, pestilential, megalomaniacal, sadomasochistic, capriciously malevolent bully." I guess Dawkins will have eternity in the lake of fire to continue to scream his remarks along with Satan. He sounds more like a man who hates God due to his physical conductions.

In 'Farewell to God,' the atheist Charles Templeton states: "The God of the Old Testament is utterly unlike the God believed in by most practicing Christians. His justice is, by modern standards, outrageous. He is biased, querulous, vindictive, and jealous of his prerogatives." Again, these could be Satan's very words to encourage a third of the angels to revolt. These two are atheists, but a better title could be Anti-God and surely Anti-Christ.

Here, we also have a description of the city of Jerusalem. John's vision and what he writes display Jerusalem in a negative light. He refers to Jerusalem as 'Sodom and Egypt and is the place of the Lord crucifixion.' We have here a great city that is figuratively called a place of lust and bondage. Jerusalem is all-important in the eyes of its Judaea occupants. It is all critical to the weak or the worldly. Sodom represents it; for the worst forms of pleasure and luxuriousness, immorality takes root. It is also Egypt, for it is the house of bondage, where the wages of sin become cruel and oppressive. Lastly, it is Jerusalem, the apostate city where the presence of Christ is hated.

At this point, we have journeyed eleven chapters into Revelation, not one mention of Rome. Much of this falsehood concerning Rome is false theology from anti-Catholic theologians who would prefer to create an erroneous interpretation rather than look for the truth. So, they promoted the idea that the Roman Catholic Church would replace the Roman Empire. It seems pretty suspicious that they would point to Rome when God does not. However, Israel and Judah are both now one nation. The nation that was and is no more at the time of the writing. Today, Israel is geographically Israel and Judah united. This unity is not necessarily the return of the twelve tribes of Israel, as we shall observe.

Zionist corrupting the Christian Doctrine, Cesar Aharon, a Jew turned Christian, aims to convert Christians to Judaism slowly. It is the fundamental goal of his "Messianic" movement. Rick Warren is another reported fake Christian corrupting American churches with his apostasy. In 1931, the Jewish Zionist leader Vladimir Jabotinski, speaking at the 5th Congress of Polish Zionist Revisionists in Warsaw, Poland, was reported in the London Times of 12/30/1931: "The Jews will become the dynamite which will blow up the British Empire." He might as well have said the Christian World, for this is what he meant; this is the Zionist movement to destroy Christianity, focusing on the Catholic Church. It is to prevent Christians from identifying the Zionist movement as evil and that the One World Order to have Jews ruling the world over the 'scum' faces of the world. In their Zionist textbook Psychopolitics, we read these words: "We have battled in America since the century's turn to bring to nothing all Christian influences, and we are succeeding. While we today seem to be kind to Christians, remember we have yet to influence the Christian world to our ends. When that is done, we will have an end to them everywhere," while Jabotinski spoke, another Jew, Genrikh Grigoryevich Yagoda, between 1931 and 1933 killed more non-Jews than Hitler would later kill Jews.

Many of today's Jewish population are not of Jacob's bloodline, but those converted to Judaism from Khazar and immigrated to Eastern Europe after the Russian invasion. This group is called Ashkenazi Jews. Some wish to make you believe that they are descendants of Jacob, but the Bible states who they are. The first mention of Ashkenazi is in Genesis 10:3, "The sons of Gomer: Ashkenaz, Riphath, and Togarmah." We can also read, "The Japhethites 5 The sons of Japheth: Gomer, Magog, Madai, Javan, Tubal, Meshek and Tiras. 6 The sons of Gomer: Ashkenaz, Riphath, and Togarmah." (Chronicles 1:6) Finally, we read in Scripture that Ashkenazi is a nation. "Lift up a banner in the land! Blow the trumpet among the nations! Prepare the nations for battle against her; summon against her these kingdoms: Ararat, Mini, and Ashkenaz. Appoint a commander against her; send up horses like a swarm of locusts." (Jeremiah 51:27)

The term Ashkenaz is the Hebrew name for the people's land known by the Assyrians as the Ishkuza. The Greeks called them Skythoi or Scythians. They were a powerful confederation of Indo-European tribes. Their language was part of the Iranian family; their original home was the steppe lands north of the Black Sea and today's southern Ukraine. This area would be part of the nation of Khazar, which also bordered Turkey.

We have examined the background of the Ashkenazi Jew now; let's take a look at Sephardic Jewry. In his letter, Paul writes, "I plan to do so when I go to Spain. I hope to see you while passing through and to have you assist me on my journey after that I have enjoyed your company for a while." (Romans 15:24 NIV) Based on this quote, we know that there had to be either a church or a synagogue in Spain. The common belief is that Paul did make the trip before finally being beheaded. Due to intellectual and trade contacts with eastern Mediterranean empires, such as Egypt and Babylonia, some of Spain's influence was prevalent in ancient Israel. Since the Phoenician civilization was an enterprising maritime trading culture spread across the Mediterranean during the first millennium BC, we can see how Israel knew of Iberia.

Shlomo ibn Virga writes a Jewish legend in Shevet Yehuda at the turn of the 16th century. It claims that Spanish kings were allies of Nebuchadnezzar and were actual participants in the siege and destruction of Jerusalem and the First Temple. It continues to report that Nebuchadnezzar transported Jews to Spain as slaves to support the Spanish." This company of Israelite exiles who are in Canaan will possess the land as far as Zarephath; the exiles from Jerusalem who are in Sepharad will possess the towns of the Negev." (Obadiah 1:20 NIV) The word Sepharad would appear to be an ancient Hebrew word for Spain. We have read Obadiah's lament over the Jewish exiles from Jerusalem, who are in Sepharad; this occurred soon after the destruction of Jerusalem and Solomon's temple by Nebuchadnezzar II. These exiled Jews were Kohanim and members of the royal family of David. Now, we have the Judaea bloodline in Spain.

Finally, we have a group known as Babylonian Judaism. While some Jews were exiled to Spain after the destruction of Jerusalem and Solomon's Temple in 588 BC by Nebuchadnezzar, the rest went to Babylon. As Jewish deportees, they were able to retain the freedom to pursue their lives as the Babylonians. However, they adopted the Aramaic languages they did to maintain their distinctive religious identity; thus, they brought the sacred scriptures with them. Babylonian Judaism did manage to adhere to the basic tenets of the Jewish faith. The belief is in one creator, God. The idea is that Israel is God's chosen people from whom the Messiah, or anointed one of God, will come to unite the Jewish people in the land of Israel and the authority of the Torah. The Rothschild family may feel that they are the anointed family that brought Israel back to its homeland.

Since the Temple was destroyed and with no sacred alter in Babylon. The community developed the Babylonian Talmud. It is a commentary on the Mishnah, a collection of rabbinic laws compiled in about 200 CE by Rabbi Judah. The Babylonian Talmud editing took place at the end of the fifth century. There are two significant components of Talmudic material. One of the Halakhah is concerned with legal and ritual matters. Two of the Aggadah, which are concerned with theological and ethical issues, are a written compendium of Rabbinic Judaism's Oral Torah and the Gemara. It contains the teachings and opinions of thousands of rabbis. Traditional Jews are required to observe the Halakhah of the Babylonian Talmud. Here, we have instructions that came out of Babylon, and it bears the name after the city and nation. It would seem to be the only real connection to the ancient city, a possible clue that may be of some importance later in our journey. Today, we have the two groups of Jews, the bloodline and the non-bloodline, reading from a book known as the Babylonian Talmud. However, the belief is that only 5% of the Jewish faith is from Jacob's bloodline. We read that the two witnesses are in Jerusalem, giving the city the moniker of Sodom and Egypt. Now, back to John's vision.

11 "But after the three and a half days, the breath of life from God entered them, and they stood on their feet, and terror struck those who saw them. 12 Then they heard a loud voice from heaven saying to them, 'Come up here.' And they went up to heaven in a cloud, while their enemies looked on. 13 At that very hour, there was a severe earthquake, and a tenth of the city collapsed. Seven thousand people were killed in the earthquake, and the survivors were terrified and gave glory to the God of Heaven. 14 The second woe has passed; the third woe is coming soon."

The two witnesses were killed and resurrected after three and a half days; then, an earthquake destroyed seven thousand people in Jerusalem. I doubt very much that they are Italians living in Vatican City. Again, we read that there is a chronological order to the events in Revelation. Two woes have passed. After seven thousand people died from an earthquake in Jerusalem, we first indicate survivors being terrified to give God glory. The fact that they were scared suggests that these were nonbelievers who woke up from their non-belief. There are three woes; these are three final chances for nonbelievers to repent

Here is what happened to Korah when he opposed Moses. It is similar to those who oppose the two witnesses. "As soon as he finished saying all this, the ground under them split apart 32, and the earth opened its mouth and swallowed them and their households, and all those associated with Korah, together with their possessions. 33 They went down alive into the realm of the dead, with everything they owned; the earth closed over them, and they perished and were gone from the community." (Numbers 16: 32) In the book of Numbers, we see the foreshadowing of the Revelation event. In both cases, those who opposed the prophet of God, the earth swallows them.

A quick overview of Jesus Christ, the Lamb God, who is worthy, has opened the scroll and removed the seven seals. Six angels have sounded their trumpets to announce an event. One, perhaps, of the six angels has already blasted a trumpet. Therefore, the remaining are still in our future. Several things are evident; there is no mention of a rapture thus far, nor do we have any evidence that points to Rome for anything. God's Drama is still fixed, with the same setting where Adam and Eve settled, in the area that became known as Babylon. Let us return to the theatre to view what is about to occur.

The Seventh Trumpet

15 "The seventh angel sounded his trumpet, and there were loud voices in heaven, which said: 'The kingdom of the world has become the Kingdom of our Lord and his Messiah, and He will reign forever and ever.'" Now, it is official, much like a presidential election. It is not official until the swearing-in of the newly elected into office.16 "And the twenty-four elders, who were seated on their thrones before God, fell on their faces and worshiped God, 17 saying: 'The Seventh Trumpet! We give thanks to you, Lord God Almighty, the One who is and who was, because you have taken your great power and have begun to reign.' 18 The nations were angry, and your wrath has come. The time has come for judging the dead and for rewarding your servants, the prophets, and your people who revere your name, both great and small—and for destroying those who destroy the earth. 19 Then God's temple in Heaven was opened, and within His temple was seen the Ark of His Covenant. And there came flashes of lightning, rumblings, peals of thunder, an earthquake, and a severe hailstorm. "

There was a quick scene change from Jerusalem to Heaven, where the angel sounded the trumpet. This trumpet sounds like the victory call. The Kingdom of the World has come, the Kingdom of our Lord and his Messiah, and he will reign forever and ever. The time has come for judging. Once this trumpet sounds, the time for repentance is over. It is the final woe. The authority of the earth is now no longer in the Dragon's hands. With this seventh trumpet sounding, the Kingdom is now in Christ's hands. The time of probating the "will" is over. Satan's illegal claim and rule over the earth are over.

I have mentioned that scripture reflects on itself through repeated sub-themes, or to put it another way, history repeats itself. Repeated themes are a more accurate interpretation. When we reflect on Joshua chapter six, we read that the Lord instructs Joshua to march around Jericho once each day for six days, sounding seven trumpets. On the seventh day, to march around seven times, sounding the trumpets and then shouting. The city's walls came down, the city took, and victory took place that day; here, with the sounding of the seventh trumpet, the wall of evil ends, and the announcement of Christ's victory.

Beasts out of the Sea & Earth

The Beast of the Sea

Here we have a similar scene as the location with the angel with the small scroll. Let's share this vision with John of the beast of the sea and earth. The two characters are in league with the dragon. The one creature that needs prayers is the dragon; this whole saga would end if the dragon would repent and surrender and accept his punishment, but he won't. He desires to take down as many as he can. He knows he cannot have the Throne in Heaven, which he lusts over. He is also jealous of man; therefore, if he cannot have the Throne and be King of kings, he desires to kill all humans who would be Christ's subjects. His blind anger and jealousy only help to send believers to Heaven.

To complete his mass genocide, he incorporates two paramount villains as evil as himself, the beast of the sea and earth. Throughout history, he has had evil subjects that have attempted to genocide races of man. Most historians and theologians would think war and murder are his forms of genocide man. However, every type of wickedness is the poison he uses to see that man ends in the lake of fire. The dragon is the ultimate sociopathic who enjoys the destruction of man. He finds pleasure in it. We see an example of this in Game of Thrones. Characters like Joffrey Baratheon and Ramsay Bolton. We look at his minions on Facebook and other social media outlets daily. When parents of a 4-year-old child suggest their child is not a boy and desires to be a girl. We need to wonder how a four-year-old discerns the difference. We see and hear in the media concerning cannibalism, rape, and murder of infants. Yet, the world of science would argue against demon possession.

Let us return to the two beasts of Revelation. These two have had many predecessors who desired world domination. Today, a man like George Soros, who claims to be a god, Jacob Rothschild, calls himself the '21st Century King of the Jews, and others have an insane plan to rule the world. These are the forefathers of these two beasts. The new world dictator uses wealth, not military power, to control the world — Zionist dictators who wish to enslave all non-Jewish people.

We notice that John's instruction is to write down what he sees. He does not call someone the Anti-Christ, but the 'beast of the sea' and the other arc villain the 'beast of the earth.' These characters are not a federal government, but like Rothschild, who controls world leaders with his wealth. When these two evil characters arrive is not clear. However, by the end of the trumpet events claiming to end the disasters, if people worship him, it is more than likely. We will see that they are only in a position of power for 42 months before Christ's return.

(13) "The dragon stood on the shore of the sea. And I saw a beast coming out of the sea. It had ten horns

and seven heads, with ten crowns on its horns, and on each head a blasphemous name. 2 The beast I saw resembled a leopard but had feet like those of a bear and a mouth like that of a lion. The dragon gave the beast his power and his throne and great authority. 3 One of the heads of the beast seemed to have had a fatal wound, but the fatal wound had been healed. The whole world was filled with wonder and followed the beast. 4 People worshiped the dragon because he had given authority to the beast, and they also worshiped the beast and asked, 'Who is like the beast? Who can wage war against it?'"

Before we start this examination of this beast, set a slide of all prior knowledge of what you may have read, heard, or seen because we will take a fresh, modern, common-sense look at this beast without any bias. I often remark that some people don't know how to read, if they read at all. Oh! They can read the words, but they don't comprehend what they read. Others overlook putting a different spin on it. Some people look through scripture and take things out of context to express their agenda. Finally, some listen to 60-second sound bites and believe it to be true when they experience deception.

First, the dragon gives this beast of the sea his power, throne, and complete authority. The dragon's throne is invisible to the human eye, and Jesus stated it is in Pergamum, Turkey. Theologians claim they moved Satan's Temple of Zeus to Germany as if the building is Satan, while his invisible throne is in the spirit world. Second, the beast appears from the sea, a metaphor for a race of people other than Israelites.

The character may not be from Turkey, but his power will.

Let's pause a moment to examine the number seven that it represents in the Bible. It is divine perfection, totality, or completion prophecies at least 490 times, or we can say seven times 70. It would suggest that the sea beast is the final individual to seek total world domination and become King of the World. The number ten is used 242 times in the Bible and symbolizes perfection. Today, the meaning continues when we say that someone is a "10," meaning perfect. Now we have ten crowns, representing the consecrated role of its wearer, in this case, the complete and ideal king. It reflects his lofty position, but on each of his heads is the blasphemous name. The word blasphemy means impious utterance concerning God or sacred things.

Therefore, the seven blasphemies' utterances or actions are against God's seven virtues; this is one evil, wicked individual, the physical embodiment of Satan. Finally, the horns' symbolism is emblems of power, dominion, glory, and fierceness, as they are the first manner of attacking and defending by animals endowed with them. Hence, this would signify the power of the beast of the sea to be absolute by his ten horns. (Daniel 8:5 Daniel 8:9; 1 Samuel 2:1; 1 Samuel 16:1 1 Samuel 16:13; 1 Kings 1:39; 22:11; Joshua 6:4 Joshua 6:5; Psalms 75:5 Psalms 75:10; 132:17; Luke 1:69)

We just read that the beast has seven heads, and it 'seemed to have had a fatal wound on one of the heads, but the deadly wound healed. The keyword here is 'seemed,' which means it is more than likely a false injury. We could say that this beast is a federation of members from three nations with a council of seven members, and one of them seems to get injured, but the wound heals. The one who is wounded will lead the others; this would be incorrect. It would also have to assume that seven men each blaspheming God differently. One could also suggest that the council could consist of members of one wealthy family.

Some theologians say that the seven heads are seven kingdoms, and the one wounded is Rome, and it heals by becoming the Roman Catholic Church. If you buy into the theory that Rome is the injured head, you need to consider that it is anti-Catholic nonsense. There is no objective evidence from John's Revelation suggesting this theory, and we shall soon see why.

One can only speculate what role he plays behind the scenes to create division between Christians. Catholicism was illegal in England for 354 years, which was the cause of many of the wars between Ireland and England. More importantly, the Catholic Church is not a government. If you choose to believe this false theology, Rome's nation had two capitals, Rome and Istanbul, and both on seven hills. However, this is not restoration because moving the capital city was a choice by the Emperor, and the Eastern Capital lasted until 1453. Therefore, it does not justify the term 'seemed to be wounded.' Some non-Catholic theologians like to heal a wound by replacing the organ with a transplant, but the word 'seemed' would be used out of context. Therefore, moving the capital is not a logical answer, nor is turning a government into a church a fake wound. Also, the verse speaks of who would wage war against it. Hence, the church has no army, not a church, which is not a kingdom in the first place. Later in Revelation, we shall witness the casting of the beasts into the lake of fire alive. Therefore it cannot be a church or a kingdom but a person.

Let's look at the image and see if it provides evidence of the character's identity. Another explanation could be the beast with three nations' ancestry, with seven characteristics, and one is flawed and corrected. The beast will appear to have the Seven Spirits of the Lord because, like the dragon, he is the master of deception. People will see him as if he has "The Spirit of the Lord resting on him— the Spirit of wisdom, and understanding, the Spirit of counsel and might, the Spirit of the knowledge and fear of the Lord—3 and he will delight in fear of the Lord. He will not judge by what he sees with his eyes or decide by what he hears with his ears." (Isaiah 11:2-3 NIV)

Notice, I said people would see him as if he has these spiritual qualities since he is the master of deception. His wound could be the loss of one of them, but heals from a hostile media remark. Finally, the beast of the earth proclaims that he is God. You may say that his wound resulted from a strike by a sword, but he has seven heads, so the sword must be a symbol, just as the seven heads, since one of the seven virtues is a fear of the Lord. He will first appear to fear the Lord, but once he proclaims to be God, the fear vanishes, and therefore he heals. Let's return to the action on the stage to witness what John sees.

5 "The beast was given a mouth to utter proud words and blasphemies and to exercise its authority for

forty-two months. 6 It opened its mouth to blaspheme God and to slander his name and his dwelling place and those who live in Heaven. 7 It was given power to wage war against God's holy people and to conquer them. And it was given authority over every tribe, people, language, and nation. 8 All inhabitants of the earth will worship the beast—all whose names have not been written in the Lamb's book of life, the Lamb who was slain from the creation of the world." 9 "Whoever has ears, let them hear. 10 'If anyone is to go into captivity, into captivity, they will go. If anyone is to be killed with the sword, with the sword, they will be killed.' This calls for patient endurance and faithfulness on the part of God's people."

Everything stops on the stage for a moment, and a narrator speaks. This statement does not suggest that believers will not be present; it suggests just the opposite. I suggest you reread it, 'If anyone is to go into captivity, into captivity, they will go. If anyone is to be killed with the sword, with the sword, they will be killed.' It calls for patience, endurance, and faithfulness of God's people. The notion of a massive rapture is a false doctrine developed by John Nelson Darby in 1830. No doubt, part of Satan's anti-Christian movement. The truth is a trial by fire and not rescued to Heaven. 'These trials will show that your faith is genuine. It is being tested as fire tests and purifies gold, though your faith is far more precious than mere gold. So when your faith remains strong through many trials, it will bring you much praise and glory and honor on the day when Jesus Christ is revealed to the whole world.' (1 Peter 1:7 NLT)

The narrator continues with a new hypothesis on the image of the beast of the sea. Let's begin by thinking that a beast is a single person. First, even in John's time, someone may have asked, "How would you breed such a creature?" You may consider breeding a lion with a leopard since they are both cats; getting that mixed-breed creature to mate with a bear would be a little more complicated. After generations of trying, you finally succeed in giving birth to one. The seven heads are seven spirits that describe his character. We need to ask this question: What understanding do we have today that John didn't but would provide us with the same outcome? The answer is DNA. The beast from the sea would have an ancestry background that would resemble these three animals. Based on today's symbols, we would have English, Russian, and German DNA for this creature, but John wrote Revelation nearly two thousand years ago.

Could a different meaning for this beast be possible? For example, one's family migrated from Russia to Germany and finally ended up in England. It would be a reasonably good possibility, but would it provide an ancestry background that could go back a couple of thousand years? Examples could be Babylon, the lion, Medo-Persia, the bear; and Greece, the Leopard. Today, this DNA could be found in Turkey, Syria, Iran, Iraq, Israel, or even in America, and the lion could represent the tribe of Judah. He could fit the description of the Mahdi. Someone with a Muslim background, but the Bible is a history of the relationship between God and the descendants of Abraham, Jacob, and David, the nation of Israel, and finally of Judah.

Our second example could be the ancestral bloodline before the family's migration. Since the Babylonians occupied Israel, a son of Judah's tribe, the lion migrated to Babylon. Later a descendant, as a result of Persia occupation, takes a Persian bribe. Finally, another inherits DNA from a Greek. Intermarriage is providing the DNA. The family migrated to Khazar, now Russia, then to Germany, and finally England. As a result, this beast is born. At first glance, a very wealthy family would fit this description: wealthy Khazarian Jews who moved to Germany and then England. This family is so rich that they can finance both sides of a war and have done just that, so who would go to war against them? Also, they own more than half the world's wealth and dictate policy in every nation using their wealth, so who would make war against them? Keep this in mind also that Khazarian descendent Jews are not Hebrew. Only God knows the actual bloodline of the beast of the sea. The media is in this very same family; it will keep us from learning the sea beast's true identity. He will be Jewish by Faith but not of an actual bloodline.

A brief statement concerning Rome had two symbols: the eagle and the other is a she-wolf nursing two infants. These two symbols do not appear in Daniel or here in Revelation. Some would suggest that the beast represents the Roman Catholic Church, but the church's logo is P and X, a Greek shorthand for Christ. The Roman Catholic Church also uses the symbol of a Lamb with a Cross. I see no evidence that would make the Roman Catholic Church the suspect of being the beast as a nation or the Pope as the beast of the sea, for that matter. Those who propose this are sure to be fooled when the evil creature arrives. Therefore, none of these symbols represent Rome. Since my personal DNA is Roman, Greek, Hebrew, and Arabic, you would picture a logo for me to be the body of a leopard, with wings of an eagle, the face of a Lion, with legs of a goat, or some other combination.

I had finished writing this chapter when I began to read First and Second Kings. I found something fascinating in 1 Kings 7:25: the use of the word Sea for a large basin with twelve bronze bulls, three in each direction, holding the bowl on their backs. Now the notion came to me that the beast coming out of the Sea could very well mean that he comes out of the basin after a purification ritual. If we continue to consider the beast of the Sea's image as his DNA, then a Khazarian Jew appears. Ashkenazi Jews, with no pure Hebrew bloodline after the construction of the New Temple, would enter into this basin for purification. Since he is not a real Israelite, John's symbolism takes it into account by referring him to the sea meaning, not of Israel's offspring, and the purification ritual. The thing that strikes me is the idea of the ceremony. It would be a sign that the beast begins his reign by appearing to be pure. The narration ends, and the scene on the stage starts again, and we hear John speak. It would be similar to the Baptism of Jesus by John the Baptist, Satan's act of deception duplication.

The Beast of the Earth

We are possibly still at the exact location where the beast has come out of the sea, but he now has a beast come from the earth.

11 "Then I saw a second beast coming out of the earth. It had two horns like a lamb, but it spoke like a dragon. 12 It exercised all the authority of the first beast on its behalf and made the earth and its inhabitants worship the first beast, whose fatal wound had been healed. 13 And it performed great signs, even causing fire to come down from heaven to the earth in full view of the people. 14 Because of the signs it was given power to perform on behalf of the first beast, it deceived the inhabitants of the earth. It ordered them to set up an image in honor of the beast who was wounded by the sword and yet lived. 15 The second beast was given power to give breath to the image of the first beast so that the image could speak and cause all who refused to worship the image to be killed. 16 It also forced all people, great and small, rich and poor, free and slave, to receive a mark on their right hands or on their foreheads, 17 so that they could not buy or sell unless they had the mark, which is the name of the beast or the number of its name. 18 This calls for wisdom. Let the person who has insight calculate the number of the beast, for it is the number of a man. That number is 666."

Here is where the Interactive Audience needs to stop the action on the stage to examine the introduction. Our examination has eliminated the idea that the sea's beast is not a government or a church. Instead, here we see confirmation that the beast of the sea is a person because the earth's beast creates an idol in his image and causes it to speak.

The Bible is a Dramatic Saga between God and a particular bloodline of people that became a nation, offsprings of Seth. Through this bloodline, Jesus enters as the Savior of humanity. The majority of the same ancestry and its offshoots rejected Him. His tribe and those of His clan reject Him. Just like in the days of Noah, his aunts, uncles, brothers, sisters, and cousins, in short, his family, those of his clan and tribe who were wicked, thought him to be a fool to build an ark that took 100 years to build. His sons may have had a hard time believing in their father. As a result, one son cursed; another fathered a nation of unbelievers. The same was true with Jesus. How many from his tribe believed Him? Probably not many from the tribe of Levi, who made up the priesthood.

We often overlook the fact that members of Christ's own extended family rejected him. Those of the tribe of Judah were Christ's kin. How often do we see or hear family members not speaking to one another because of different beliefs? I know of two cousins; one is a believer in Christ, and the other in reincarnation. The one who believes in rebirth mocks her cousin, claiming she believes in a myth and she is foolish for believing in such a falsehood. While the other loves her cousin and wants her to come to the Lord to have eternal life. The difference, however, is that one mocks while the other loves. The irony is the one who claims to believe in reincarnation does not even practice her faith well. Even in reincarnation, to evolve to a higher state of being, you must demonstrate love, much like the Levites who were the priests and rejected Jesus. Their ancestors had tried to overthrow Moses and Aaron, and now what their ancestors decided to do to Moses, they did to Jesus.
The Israelites gathered together against Moses and Aaron. They said to them, "You take too much upon yourselves, for all the congregation is holy, every one

of them, and the Lord is among them. Why then do you exalt yourselves above the assembly of the Lord?" (Number 16:3 NKJV)

The same tribe rebels once again, this time against Jesus. The irony is that a member of their own will be the one to destroy them. The people of the Jewish faith have long awaited a Messiah. They rejected the true Messiah, but they will welcome the 'false messiah,' the beast of the sea. Non-Catholic theologians are obsessed with making a Catholic Pope the beast of the sea or earth. So they overlook a simple requirement: the Jewish faith leaders will never accept a Christian of any kind, even a bad one, to be their Messiah.

God's saga continues with Gentiles becoming an addition to the vine, but the story remains between God and His covenant people. The Bible tells us of a love story between God and the unfaithful nation of Israel. The Drama ends with a New Jerusalem and with the same key people. The Israeli bloodline is the protagonist of the Drama and, in many ways, the tragic hero. Over and over again, it falls victim to the deception of the antagonist, the supervillain Satan. Throughout the Drama, the protagonist, the offspring of the 12 tribes, has turned on God. This misleading leads to their demise; the protagonist becomes the antagonist who destroys himself, the tragic hero. From Exodus to Jesus Christ, Jacob's descendants have turned their backs on God perhaps 100 times or more. A reading of the book of Judges will have you see just how often they manage to rebel. During this period, God permits them to govern themselves, much like what takes place between Christ and the present. The Israelites no sooner leave Egypt than they build an idol to worship.

The picture we see repeated throughout the Bible is of various characters and themes that repeat. The roles and themes of those in the Garden of Eden. Therefore, the Drama began with the Dragon, a serpent, Eve, and Adam. It concludes with the same Dragon. The snake represents the beast of the sea and earth, while Eve is now the Harlot. Eve spreads the serpent's word, 'partake of this,' and Adam, the blind fool who followed along, is now the blind population. Therefore, the end players are all from Adam's bloodline, through Noah, through Jacob, and his 12 sons. From the beginning to the Drama's end, it is the Saga of God and His relationship with a particular tribe of people. The main characters are all from the same bloodline. Keep in mind that all of the tribes of Judaea are related to Jesus.

Let's examine the image of a sheep for the beast of the earth. First, we must consider where do we see the mention of a sheep. "Abel also brought an offering--fat portions from some of the firstborn of his flock. The Lord looked with favor on Abel and his offering." (Genesis 4:4). There are some 55 verses concerning sheep in the Bible. Here, we now have a sheep with two horns, and it speaks like a dragon. Meaning this sheep is not pure but evil and has power. Also, it comes out of the earth, meaning it is one nation. The first beast came out of the sea, a mixture of several different animals. This beast is only a sheep, meaning from one country, one root, one form of DNA. Since the Bible deals predominately with Israel, they have offered the sheep, a lamb, to God. Christ is the sacrificial lamb that they rejected. Therefore, this lamb represents the false prophet, the lamb they will accept. I will repeat this vital fact: he will need to be Jewish because they will not follow Goyim, a foreigner, as their prophet or a messiah.

Throughout the history of Israel and even before, prophets have served Kings and Pharaoh. Twenty prophets served the Kings of Israel, starting with Saul and ending with Malachi. The Pharisees and the Sadducee served Herod the Great, who was Edomite. They also helped the Emperors of Rome. In the final hours of this world, a false prophet from Israel will serve an evil Leader. He also will have some Israelite blood in his veins and be a 'King, President, or Dictator' as it has occurred before. History repeats itself. When we examine world history, we find that from Joseph to the present, the Israelite people have managed to enter into political positions of other nations when they are in exile. Today, they own most federal banks worldwide, media, and publishing houses, with many of them in government leadership positions.

It is also interesting that they have destroyed the nation where they reside once in a position of power. Historians ignore why the tribes of Jacob became slaves in Egypt. Joseph gave his brothers a better portion of the land and provided them with food while he slowly brought the Egyptians into slavery to purchase food. Later, a new Pharaoh changes things. We see this occur throughout history, and today, much of today's wealth, power, and media influence are in their control. "For the Lord, your God will bless you as he has promised, and you will lend to many nations but will borrow from none. You will rule over many nations, but none will rule over you." (Deuteronomy 15:6 NIV) They have been ruling behind the scenes since the destruction of the First Temple.

People seem to forget one critical point the whole book of the Bible is about the promise God made to Seth, Noah, Abraham, Jacob, Moses, and David, and the covenants he made with them and their descendants. God is always punishing Israel for turning its back on Him. God rescues the Israelites from bondage in Egypt, and as soon as Moses leaves to talk with God, they build an idol to worship. (Exodus 32) God tells Israel to turn from idol worship. "Therefore say to the people of Israel, 'This is what the Sovereign Lord says: Repent! Turn from your idols and renounce all your detestable practices!'" (Ezekiel 14:6 NIV). The fulfillment of God's promise to these people is in the Son of David. Jesus is not from a Greek or a Roman offspring but an Israelite, Judah's tribe. Yes, we read that Israel is occupied by other nations, but as a result of their wickedness. II Kings 17:7-8 speaks of the sins of the Kingdom of Israel. "For so it was that the children of Israel had sinned against the Lord their God, who had brought them up out of the land of Egypt, and they had feared other gods and had walked in the statutes of the nations whom the Lord had cast out from before the children of Israel."

I could write a book about all the times Israel turned its back on God, over 100 times, and maybe I will. Its ultimate crime was when Israel's leaders turned their backs on their Messiah, the Son of God, as a result of the destruction of the Temple in 70 AD. Hence, God scatters them throughout the world. In the end, Israelites will turn once more to worship an idol and a demon in place of the Lord. After all the times they have turned their back on God, they will do it again. An expression is, "If something happens once, it may never happen again, but if it happens twice is surely to happen a third time."

There is an unholy trinity, a counterfeit, of God's Holy Trinity, the 'dragon god,' the beast of the sea, the false messiah, and the beast of the earth as the holy spirit. This false prophet will use technology, make an image speak, use fraudulent means to make the first beast appear wounded, and later make it seem that he rose from the dead, for only a prophet filled with the spirit of God can bring a dead man to life. Christ, who holds the key to life and death, is not a false son of man, a child of Satan. The present young people have already become addicted to technology. They seem stuck to their smartphones. They are fed fake news, fake science, and even false religious doctrine daily. I would not be surprised if, from the dark web, people receive hidden subliminal messages.

The beast of the sea will be Jewish because the Jewish leaders will not accept a non-Jew as their Messiah. They did not accept Jesus, and he was from the House of David from Judah's tribe. The Lake of Fire will become a lake of ice before receiving a Gentile as a Messiah. The beast of the sea will attempt to create a one-world nation ruled from Jerusalem. The false prophet uses the media to spread the deception of the beast of the sea; this is presently taking place. The immediate objective is to destroy America. Most people will overlook this possible detail, but the media's voice could be a woman, a Jezebel, or a Harlot. She would represent her ancestor Eve, who gave to her husband to eat, and the people an image of Adam, the foolish follower.

Assuming that it would be a man, 20 prophets in the Bible advised Kings who were both Israeli and non-Israeli. Since this repeated track is recorded, why would God suddenly change and go outside of the Israelite community for a Gentile? He wouldn't. We must stick with the storyline that through Abraham, through the descendants of Jacob, Seth's bloodline is the protagonist in the saga. The Gentiles play a sub role and even surpass the Israelites in maintaining a relationship with God. One who has eyes to see and ears to hear can recognize that the spirit of the future beast of the earth is already upon us. Look at how today's media spews nothing but lies and deception; President Trump has labeled it fake news. Observe how the media and the government of America spread lies and deceit, and notice who owns the press and pulls strings behind the scenes to produce an anti-Christian agenda.

Here is the only time that I will move an event before another. John the Baptist announced the coming of the Lord. The media may begin to proclaim an individual's great character and potential as he arrives on the scene. Look at how they have glorified Barak Obama. Some of the dumbest videos on YouTube claim that the Pope will announce himself as the Anti-Christ. The last thing the dragon, the master of deception, will do is tell you his evil son has arrived, nor will he say, "Hi, I am the Anti-Christ you have been waiting for." Soros announced that he is a god because he creates things, but that isn't saying I am the evil anti-Christ. However, he is evil, and he isn't a Christian, making him an anti-Christ. With that statement that he is a god, we need to consider his state of mind. One must ask why isn't the Jewish community calling him a blasphemer.

The False Messiah will make no declaration. The Beast of the Sea is present, then the Beast of the Earth will come on the scene and begin to promote the great one, much like the media did with Obama. I keep getting the impression that the beast of the earth owns the press, and Jezebel is the female anchorperson on a news channel, with a broad viewing audience spewing the deception as a woman expels her menstruation. Listen to the vile monologue that spews from the mouths of the women on the View.

Let us also examine the nature of the real Jew and false Jewish Zionists. The real Jews believe it will reveal the One God in the Torah. It affirms Divine Providence and, accordingly, views Jewish exile as a punishment for sin. The Torah Jew believes redemption may be achieved solely through prayer and penance. Judaism calls upon all Jews to obey the Torah in its entirety, including the commandment to be patriotic citizens.

The Zionist, the false Jew, rejects the Creator, His Revelation, and reward and punishment. Here are the beliefs and the fruit of the beast of the earth. Zionists have persecuted the Palestinian people and the spiritual and physical endangering of the Jewish people. It was these very Zionist that supported Hitler. The Rothschild financed both sides of World War 1 and 2. Zionists encourage treasonous, dual loyalty among unsuspecting Jews throughout the world. At its root,

Zionism sees reality as barren and desacralized. It is the antithesis of Torah Judaism.

The Neturei Karta International, Jew United Against Zionism, has stated a vile lie that stalks the Jewish people worldwide. They claim that the myth is so reprehensible, so far from the truth, that it can only gain popularity through the cooperation of powerful forces in the "mainstream" media and educational establishment, both of which are owned by wealthy Zionists. This group claims that this lie has brought many innocent people to untold suffering. If unchecked, it has the potential to create extraordinary tragedy in the future, this lie that declares that Judaism and Zionism are identical. As we have already seen, it is further from the truth.

Judaism is the belief in revelation at Sinai. It is the belief that exile is a punishment for Jewish sins. Zionism, on the other hand, has, for over a century, denied Sinaitic revelation. It believes that Jewish exile can end with military aggression, and we see that in the Middle East. Since before World War One, Zionism has strategically dispossessed the Palestinian people, who lived in harmony with real believing Jews. It has ignored the Palestinians' claims and subjected them to persecution, torture, and death.

Neturei Karta International has maintained that Torah Jews worldwide are shocked and hurt at this short-lived dogma of non-religious and cruelty. Thousands of Torah scholars and saints have condemned this movement from its inception. They knew that the pre-existing relationship between Jews and Muslims in the Holy Land was bound to suffer as Zionism advanced. Neturei Karta has stood at the forefront of the battle against Zionism for over a century. They continue to claim that the so-called "State of Israel" stands rejected on religious grounds by the Torah. Its monstrous insensitivity to the laws of basic decency and fairness appalls all men, be they Jewish or not. Their presence refutes the base lie that the evil, Zionism, represents the Jewish people, while the reverse is true.

Members of the Neturei Karta are sad, day in and day out, at the terrible death toll emanating from the Holy Land. Not one of them would have occurred if Zionism had not unleashed its evil energies upon the world. As faithful, righteous Jews, the NKI believes Jews are called upon to live in peace and harmony with all men. God advises the Jews to be law-abiding and patriotic citizens in all lands. God ordains them to be an example of righteous living for other nations.

The NKI condemns the current Zionist atrocities in the Holy Land. This organization yearns for peace based on mutual respect. Their conviction is that the proposed mutual respect is doomed to fail as long as the Israeli Nation exists. Here we have righteous Torah-practicing Jews who would welcome the abolition of the Nation of Israel peacefully. I believe that these Torah-believing Jews will one day come to know Christ. They will be worthy of real redemption when all men join together in fellowship with Christ and become brotherhood in His worship.

Theologians' false teachings will have people looking for the beasts of the sea and earth in another area because the dragon has deceived them as he deceived Eve so long ago. The serpent only had to change one word in a sentence to cause that deception, and the word was "not". The dragon has encouraged so many theologians to look in another direction. These theologians have missed the origin and true identity of the beast of sea and earth. They seem to ignore the fact that both Jews and Muslims reject Jesus/Yeshua as the Son of God. Therefore, many will be caught by surprise when they suddenly find that the beasts are upon them. It will shake their belief because they had believed with all their heart that they were right and discover just how wrong they have been.

The Zionists are working behind the scenes. They have even made it illegal to speak against those of the Jewish faith so they could hide behind them. When they can care less about those who are Jewish believers of the Torah, the evidence is there for those who seek the truth, but soon, the fact will no longer be available. Zuckerberg has already begun to screen postings on FaceBook. The Zionist movement is the authentic voice of the Beast of the Earth. People need to ask why so many Jewish American politicians oppose Trump when he supports Israel and other nations to create peace in the Middle East. Let us pray for Christ's return.

The Lamb and the 144,000

The scene changes to Mount Zion, one of the Seven Hills that is the foundation for Jerusalem. Here we witness, with John, a large crowd.

(14) "Then I looked, and there before me was the Lamb, standing on Mount Zion, and with him 144,000 who had His name and His Father's name written on their foreheads. 2 And I heard a sound from heaven like the roar of rushing waters and like a loud peal of thunder. The sound I heard was like that of harpists playing their harps. 3 And they sang a new song before the throne and before the four living creatures and the elders, no one could learn the song except the 144,000 who had been redeemed from the earth. 4 These are those who did not defile themselves with women, for they remained virgins. They follow the Lamb wherever He goes. They were purchased from among mankind and offered as first fruits to God and the Lamb. 5 No lie was found in their mouths; they are blameless."

This sentence gave me a reason to examine, "They were purchased from among mankind and offered as first-fruits to God and the Lamb." The first fruits of the harvest were an offering to the priests. The firstborn son of each human male belongs to God. We know that the firstborn males of Egypt died. (Exodus 11:5 NIV) The first fruits of animals were sacrificed. Jesus is the firstborn Son of God, who is a sacrifice. The fact the word offered is in use here does not imply in any way rapture, but more likely, they perished as young Jewish Christ-believing males while still virgins.

Once again, I wish to quote from Jude 1:14, who is also quoting Enoch the seventh from Adam. Enoch prophesied of this, saying, "Behold, the Lord cometh with ten thousands of his saints, to execute judgment upon all, and to convince all that are ungodly among them of all their ungodly deeds which they have ungodly committed, and of all their hard speeches which ungodly sinners have spoken against Him."

What John has witnessed is a future event, and he describes it in a literal form; there is nothing symbolic of seeing Christ with His army. What is interesting in this scene is that the stage is in two parts. First, we can see with John, Jesus with His army on Mount Zion, and the four creatures with the elders before the Throne of God.

Here is another example of something in an earlier chapter reappearing. John has seen the 144,000 in Heaven. Now he sees them on Mount Zion, with the Lord Jesus Christ. At this point in God's Drama, people in Jerusalem cannot witness the Lord and the 144,000 standing on Mount Zion, the highest point in ancient Jerusalem. Just as in the day when Elisha prayed, "Open his eyes, Lord, so that he may see." 'Then the Lord opened the servant's eyes, and he looked and saw the hills full of horses and chariots of fire all around Elisha' (2 Kings 6:17). John can witness this scene, but no one else because it is a future event even for me at the time of the writing.

Here, we also have a King with his army standing on a high point to survey the strategy and prepare for the upcoming battle. Jesus is standing on one of the seven hills of Jerusalem. I wonder if Jesus once again recalls Himself saying, "Jerusalem, Jerusalem, you who kill the prophets and stone those sent to you, how often I have longed to gather your children together, as a hen gathers her chicks under her wings, and you were not willing." He may also recall saying, "Look, your house is left to you desolate. I tell you, you will not see me again until you say, Blessed is he who comes in the name of the Lord." (Luke 13:34-35 NIV)

Many, at this point, still will not believe it. So the next recollections, as Jesus stands, there is, "I tell you, If they remain silent, the very stones will cry out." As Jesus approached Jerusalem and saw the city, He wept over it and said, "If only you had known on this day what would bring you peace! But now it is hidden from your eyes." (Luke 19 40-42NIV) It is hidden from the eyes of the Israelis, first and to the Gentile nonbelievers as well.

The Lord and His army can see for miles from this high point. The King is preparing the strategy for the battle that is about to ensue. The dragon's defeat in Heaven, and now comes the final hour where the dragon slayer, the Lord Jesus Christ, will end Satan and his rule. Again we find the location to be in the Western area of Nebuchadnezzar's Kingdom Babylon. In Jerusalem, where the Jewish leaders rejected Jesus, the Zionist Jews are still rejecting Jesus and God the Father.

The Three Angels

We are still viewing the scene at Mount Zion when an angel appears flying in the sky.

6 "Then I saw another angel flying in midair, and he had the eternal gospel to proclaim to those who live on the earth—to every nation, tribe, language and people. 7 He said in a loud voice, 'Fear God and give Him glory, because the hour of His judgment has come. Worship Him who made the heavens, the earth, the sea and the springs of water.'"

We hear another announcement that the time has come. God continues to let people know that time is running out. God's angel makes one more plea to fear God and give Him glory for what He has done.

8 "A second angel followed and said, 'Fallen! Fallen is Babylon the Great,' which made all the nations drink the maddening wine of her adulteries." Isn't this interesting Jesus, with His army standing on Mount Zion, one of the seven hills of Jerusalem? This same mount was once part of Babylon. The city of Babylon was also built on seven hills. However, Jesus is about to attack with His army from this city with seven hills. It is here where the angels say, "Babylon has fallen." He is speaking of Jerusalem.

Jesus is standing with his army on Mount Zion in Jerusalem, about to attack. He is not standing on Mount Aventino in Rome. If Rome is the fallen city of Babylon, as many false Christian teachers claim, why is Jesus, King of kings on Mount Zion, ready to attack Jerusalem? If Rome was his target, the answer is because Rome is not. Any High School student knows from watching the Game of Thrones that you can't take Kings Landing in front of Castle Black.

9 "A third angel followed them and said in a loud voice: If anyone worships the beast and its image and receives its mark on their forehead or on their hand, 10 they, too, will drink the wine of God's fury, which has been poured full strength into the cup of His wrath. They will be tormented with burning sulfur in the presence of the holy angels and of the Lamb. 11 And the smoke of their torment will rise forever and ever. There will be no rest day or night for those who worship the beast and its image, or for anyone who receives the mark of its name. 12 This calls for patient endurance on the part of the people of God who keep his commands and remain faithful to Jesus."

Let's take a moment to review this scene. First, John sees Christ with an army of 144,000 standing on Mount Zion in Jerusalem, the western territory of Babylon. He then sees three angels flying overhead in the sky. The angels each make an announcement. The first says, "Fear God and give Him glory because the hour of his judgment has come. Worship Him who made the heavens, the earth, the sea, and the springs of water."

The King of kings is on Mount Zion in Jerusalem, a city built on seven hills, and here is where the hour finally comes. The second angel claims, "Fallen! Fallen is Babylon the Great!" Christ is standing on a mount in Jerusalem, so Jesus is about to take down Jerusalem, not Vatican City. Jerusalem is a city located in the Kingdom of Babylon. Finally, the third angel proclaims, "If anyone worships the beast and its image and receive its mark on their forehead or their hand, 10 they, too, will drink the wine of God's fury."

Nothing in this part of John's vision is symbolic, except that the second angel uses the moniker of "Babylon the Great" for Jerusalem; what more fitting for a King to return to the place where He experienced rejection and punish those who rejected him. We have examined several different elements of the evil present in the territory of Babylon, including the Garden of Eden, the place of the origin of all sin.

In Nebuchadnezzar's dream, the statue represents his Kingdom and how it decays from gold to clay and, finally, the image's destruction. When we examine the religion of the Babylonians, we see a pagan society with idol worship. What is idol worship? According to Webster, it is "the worship of idols or excessive devotion to or reverence for someone or thing." Idol, therefore, is anything that replaces the one real God.

The most prevalent form of idolatry in Bible times was worshiping images embodying the various pagan deities. In this case, the idol becomes more than a means of worshipping a god; it becomes the object of worship—the god itself. "But those who trust in idols, who say to images, 'You are our gods,' will be turned back in utter shame." (Isaiah 42:17). It was the Israelites that made this statement; this happened long before the nation of Babylon.

While Moses was receiving this Commandment, the Israelites were building a Golden Calf. They proclaimed."These are your gods, Israel, who brought you up out of Egypt." (Exodus 32:4 NIV) However, God said, "You shall not make for yourself an image in the form of anything in heaven above or on the earth beneath or in the waters below. 5 You shall not bow down to them or worship them; for I, the Lord your God, am a jealous God, punishing the children for the sin of the parents to the third and fourth generation of those who hate me, 6 but showing love to a thousand generations of those who love me and keep my commandments." (Exodus 20:4-7) Here is an exciting thought: the Church in Rome and the Greek Church are still here after nearly 2 thousand years. The Temple, however, is destroyed twice, and God will destroy it a third time. It is often said, "If it happens once, it may never happen again, but if it happens twice, it surely will happen again." God destroyed the Northern Kingdom of Israel because of idol worship.

The Bible is a historical drama of a nation that continuously turns its back on its personal God to worship idols. Moses' brother is part of the rebellion. We can only speculate if it was the Israelites who caused the Babylonians to worship idols. God tells Ezekiel this: "Therefore say to the people of Israel, 'This is what the Sovereign Lord says: Repent! Turn from your idols and renounce all your detestable practices!" (Ezekiel 14:6) Throughout the Bible, the Israelites and later

Judea turn their backs on God and His Son. Today's Zionists, false Jews, do not believe in God at all. Their idol is wealth and power. They have fallen continuously from their first love and followed other lovers as an adulteress. They do as they please. They continue to worship an idol, wealth, and they cause ours to do as well.

Back to the stage, we observe John as he continues to report on what he saw.

13 "Then I heard a voice from heaven say, 'Write this: Blessed are the dead who die in the Lord from now on. Yes, says the Spirit, they will rest from their labor, for their deeds will follow them.'"

When I read this, I felt very blessed. My mother was dying from diabetes. Her doctor told my father and me that we needed to decide to remove her from life support. He said he would give us two weeks to make a decision. I went to ask her what she desired. I had her blink once for yes and twice for no. I asked her if she was at peace with God and Jesus, and she blinked once. I questioned if she was ready to go home to Christ, and she blinked once. As a result, we never had to decide because Christ took her a few days later. My heart was filled with joy when I read this because I knew of my mother's spiritual condition before she died, and I know she will be with the Lord for sure.

We come to another point where theologians seem to either ignore, overlook, or disregard altogether to promote their doctrine. It deals with the rapture. We are in the fourteenth chapter of Revelation, and we now get our first clue of it. The time of judgment has arrived. Many theologians teach the idea of a rapture taking "born again" believers to Heaven as God did with Enoch based solely on a verse spoken by Jesus in Matthew 24:40: "Two men will be in the field; one will be taken and the other left." However, here is what they leave out from the verse before, "And they were oblivious until the flood came and swept them all away. So will be the coming of the Son of Man." They all died except those in the ark who were left behind. In Genesis, Lot receives instructions, "Flee for your lives! Don't look back, and don't stop anywhere in the plain! Flee to the mountains, or you will be swept away!" Again, the phrase "swept away" is used to mean you will die. As I already mentioned, this is a false teaching that began in 1830 by John Darby. It has infected most conservative and evangelical churches and is a doctrine that the Catholic Church rejects.

The non-believing, wicked people have been swept away by the flood. It means they died. Noah is still on earth on a boat. He was not raptured to Heaven but left behind. The same is accurate with Lot. The Lord tells Lot to escape; then the Lord destroys the city. "He overthrew those cities, and all the valley, and all the inhabitants of the cities, and what grew on the ground. But his wife, from behind him, looked back, and she became a pillar of salt." (Genesis 19:25) Lot's wife dies because her heart is with the city. Lot and his two daughters are left behind, and everything he owns perishes.

Revelation tells us what happens, but first, let's reread the previous verse, 13 "Then I heard a voice from heaven say, 'Write this: Blessed are the dead who die in the Lord from now on.' Yes, says the Spirit, 'they will rest from their labor, for their deeds will follow them.'" People who die in the Lord. It does not say those who ascended into Heaven. Now, we see what God has planned. Yes, those like Noah will not be swept away and left behind; they are still here when Christ returns.

Harvesting the Earth and Trampling the Winepress

The scene changes once again, and John sees another event. It is another area where John N. Darby's doctrine of a Pre-tribulation rapture of 1830 falls apart.

14 "I looked, and there before me was a white cloud, and seated on the cloud was one like a son of man with a crown of gold on his head and a sharp sickle in his hand. 15 Then another angel came out of the temple and called in a loud voice to him who was sitting on the cloud, "Take your sickle and reap, because the time to reap has come, for the harvest of the earth is ripe." 16 So he who was seated on the cloud swung his sickle over the earth, and the earth was harvested."

You use a sickle for harvesting grain crops or cutting succulent forage chiefly for feeding livestock. My cousin in Italy still uses it today to cut tall grass to feed cows or store hay for the cows during the winter months for all the world's vegetarians. You have to kill the plant to harvest unless you are picking fruit from a tree. Therefore, there is nothing here unless you stretch the imagination to create a symbol that swinging a sharp sickle is a means to rapture people of the earth; ironically, the grim reaper (Arch Angel Azrael), the character for death, has a sickle.

After I read this chapter and before commenting on it, I had to stop and reflect on what John saw and its meaning. I like so many others, had come to believe in the disappearing act of Enoch. "Enoch walked faithfully with God; then, he was no more because God took him away." (Genesis 5:24 NIV) I often even said I couldn't wait to go the same way, but as I read Revelation once again, only without commentary, with the eye of someone who has taught reading and writing for over 20 years. I found no evidence of a rapture thus far. Therefore, the idea that God has John seeing an angel with a sickle troubled me, so I had to halt writing to understand the meaning of this image. I prayed and wrestled with the idea for nearly two days when the Lord spoke but one word, "uproot." I instantly saw a different vision of pulling a plant by its roots to be transplanted elsewhere. It was the clue I needed; the sickle cut the plant from its source. Therefore, the plant would die since it no longer had the support of life from the root. It became clear that the life was removed from the body, for it was swept away. God does not need our old bodies when He can give us a new one.

Here is another thought for those who know little or nothing about plants and planting: if the Lord had said to uproot the plants for replanting. I would see the symbol of a possible rapture. Since the plant's root gives life to the rest of the plant and a sickle cuts the plant away from the source, the only correct interpretation can be that life is no longer attached to the body; therefore, the uprooting of the plant is not taking place. Thus, transplanting from earth to Heaven, the idea of a rapture is out of place. Also, in 1 Chronicle 21:16, we read, "David looked up and saw the angel of the Lord standing between heaven and earth, with a drawn sword in his hand extended over Jerusalem." The angel is there to kill people to die from a sharp cutting tool.

1 Thessalonians 4:16: "For the Lord Himself will descend from heaven with a loud command, with the voice of an archangel, and with the trumpet of God, and the dead in Christ will be the first to rise. 17 After that, we who are alive and remain will be caught up together with them in the clouds to meet the Lord in the air, and so we will always be with the Lord." Paul is saying the dead first, not the other way around. We also just read, "Blessed are the dead who die in the Lord from now on." There is one more clue: 'We who are alive and remain,' those still alive after the punishment of the seven bowels will ascend into Heaven because God will destroy the present earth to recreate another. We will see that later in Revelation.

We watch John move to another location. Then, those of us in the audience witness a scene change that takes place in Heaven.

17 "Another angel came out of the temple in heaven, and he too had a sharp sickle. 18 Still another angel, who had charge of the fire, came from the altar and called in a loud voice to him who had the sharp sickle, 'Take your sharp sickle and gather the clusters of grapes from the earth's vine because its grapes are

ripe.' 19 The angel swung his sickle on the earth, gathered its grapes, and threw them into the great winepress of God's wrath. 20 They were trampled in the winepress outside the city, and blood flowed out of the press, rising as high as the horses' bridles for a distance of 1,600 stadia."

Here, we see the grapes cut from the vine. Anyone who has seen a vineyard knows you grow and harvest grapes every year as long as the vine is alive, so we have a death once again. Here, we see a very different picture. Not only is the grape taken from its life source, the vine, but the press is squeezing out the juice of life. Also, consider the act of the winepress is applying force to break the skin, so the liquid pours out. The symbol here represents God's wrath to exterminate the wicked, and their blood will pour out.

However, this death squeezes blood out of the bodies to a height of about six feet and 300 miles long. There is no measure of the width, but it would be safe to say more than six feet wide. Notice the angel only cuts the clusters of grapes from the vine. It is similar to the first harvest when the fruit of the plant is cut away from the source. In this case, the vine. In both cases, the plant's root was the life of the plant remains in the earth. Therefore, the symbolism here is that the body remains on the ground. The second part of the grapes harvest is that the juice is pressed out and then emptied and thrown away. Anyone who has ever made wine would not pour out good grape juice unless it was awful and not good enough to make vinegar. Concluding the investigation into the harvest, the proper interpretation is that there are two deaths: worthy and discarded.

One more clue that Darby is mistaken is from Matthew 24: 39-40, "And they were oblivious until the flood came and swept them all away. So will be the coming of the Son of Man. 40 Two men will be in the field: one will be taken and the other left. 41 Two women will be grinding at the mill: one will be taken, and the other left." The key is that everyone but Noah's wife, sons, and their wives died and swapped away. God has Noah build an Ark. God does not take him to Heaven with his body. He is left behind; this is how it will be that those who have stood fast like Noah will see the wicked perish.

Seven Angels With Seven Plagues

(15) "I saw in heaven another great and marvelous sign: seven angels with the seven last plagues—last, because with them God's wrath is completed. 2 And I saw what looked like a sea of glass glowing with fire and, standing beside the sea, those who had been victorious over the beast and its image and over the number of its name. They held harps given them by God 3 and sang the song of God's servant Moses and of the Lamb: 'Great and marvelous are your deeds, Lord God Almighty. Just and true are your ways, King of the nations. 4 Who will not fear you, Lord, and bring glory to your name? For you alone are holy. All nations will come and worship before you, for your righteous acts have been revealed.'"

5 "After this, I looked, and I saw in heaven the temple—that is, the tabernacle of the covenant law—and it was opened. 6 Out of the temple came the seven angels with the seven plagues. They were dressed in clean, shining linen and wore golden sashes around their chests. 7 Then one of the four living creatures gave to the seven angels seven golden bowls filled with the wrath of God, who lives forever and ever. 8 And the temple was filled with smoke from the glory of

God and from his power, and no one could enter the temple until the seven plagues of the seven angels were completed."

As with John's first image of the Throne of God, we need to look at this as literal. John sees seven angels and the garments they are wearing. He recognizes those who had been victorious over the beast and its image and the number of its name. Their victory is martyrdom for refusing to take the mark. They were playing their harps and singing to God. Here again, we have those who did not receive the mark of the beast. Some would suggest that the star of Solomon is the mark of the beast. The symbol for Israel, also the name of a man, is the twelve tribes' father. The reason for this logo, it is a symbol of the present flag of Israel. The emblem has six points, six lines, and six triangles; the large triangles are both equilateral, meaning that they have three angles that measure 60 degrees each, for 60, 60, 60. It would seem logical if Israel becomes the seat of the One World Order, with its capital in Jerusalem; therefore, this symbol would mark the beast. It would seem that this is the intention of the Zionist elite that controls the world's wealth. The symbol is for the nation of Israel; also, it is the name of a person; this could be the mark of the beast, but just one of many suggestions.

The Seven Bowls of God's Wrath

We are sitting in the audience, viewing the scene with John as he observes the angel's events pouring out their bowls of wrath and the result of each one. These plagues seem to mirror those of Egypt in Exodus. We continue to see here in Revelation God's continuous use of angels to do His Will. Once again, there is a conflict in what some theologians teach. Their notion is that God does all the work, but here, we see angels having their orders and carrying them out. What King does the job of his servants?

(16) "Then I heard a loud voice from the temple saying to the seven angels, 'Go, pour out the seven bowls of God's wrath on the earth.' 2 The first angel went and poured out his bowl on the land, and ugly, festering sores broke out on the people who had the mark of the beast and worshiped its image. 3 "The second angel poured out his bowl on the sea, and it turned into blood like that of a dead person, and every living thing in the sea died."

4 "The third angel poured out his bowl on the rivers and springs, of water, and they became blood. 5 Then I heard the angel in charge of the waters say: 'You are

just in these judgments, O Holy One, you who are and who were; 6 for they have shed the blood of Your holy people and Your prophets, and You have given them blood to drink as they deserve.'" Again, to point out, this reference is about Jerusalem. "Jerusalem, Jerusalem, you who kill the prophets and stone those sent to you, how often I have longed to gather your children together, as a hen gathers her chicks under her wings, and you were not willing." (Luke 13:34 NIV)

Again and again, we see reference to Jerusalem. The Roman Empire may have killed Israelites and Christians, but they did not destroy God's prophets. Since God never sent them to Rome. The holy people referenced here must be those who believed in God with all their heart and soul and in His Son. We know that the first believers in Christ were, in fact, from the tribes of Israel, and many of them, the tribe of Judah, Christ's tribesmen that believed in Him, were persecuted and killed. Based on Christ's quote, we know that Jerusalem, ruled by the tribe of Judah, had murdered the prophets. Hence, the people who deserve to drink from this plague live in Jerusalem.

7 "And I heard the altar respond: 'Yes, Lord God Almighty, true and just are your judgments.'" 8 "The fourth angel poured out his bowl on the sun, and the sun was allowed to scorch people with fire. 9 They were seared by the intense heat, and they cursed the name of God, who had control over these plagues, but they refused to repent and glorify Him!"

It would make some Liberals very happy that global warming is accurate to the point of burning skin; this would give them a reason to say, "I told you so," but they will not recognize the actual source. It won't be manmade or even cow flatulence, but the Will of God.

10 "The fifth angel poured out his bowl on the throne of the beast, and its kingdom was plunged into darkness. People gnawed their tongues in agony 11 and cursed the God of heaven because of their pains and their sores, but they refused to repent of what they had done."

Many will disagree with this statement. However, in a later chapter, you will see why Jerusalem is the city where the beast's throne resides. Jerusalem will be the capital of the NWO. It is not the seat of the throne of Satan, which has a location in Pergamum. The Zionist Jewish dream is to be the race that rules the world. President Trump has declared Jerusalem the capital of Israel.

12 "The sixth angel poured out his bowl on the great River Euphrates, and its water was dried up to prepare the way for the kings from the East."

Here again, the River Euphrates is a location for an event in Revelation. Due to this river's constant appearance, it is clear that God wants us to be sure of where the majority of occurrences will spring fort. Notice the river here is not the Tiber, which flows through the city of Rome. Some theologians think God doesn't know one river from another, but I believe He knows that the Euphrates do not flow out of Italy's Apennine Mountains. I guess it isn't their fault since schools don't teach geography today, or perhaps the false teachers of scriptures don't want to know the real identity of the Harlot and that of the beasts. They will argue that it is the Roman Empire through the Roman Catholic Church. If that were so, why would you need an army to combat a church?

13 "Then I saw three impure spirits that looked like frogs; they came out of the mouth of the dragon, out of the mouth of the beast, and out of the mouth of the false prophet. 14 They are demonic spirits that perform signs, and they go out to the kings of the whole world to gather them for the battle on the great day of God Almighty."

Here is a fascinating sign: John sees a demon frog come out of the mouth of the dragon. It seems like a scene from 'Ghostbusters,' slimy creatures that resemble frogs coming out of these three creatures. These spirits coming out of the dragon, a fallen angel, a spirit being, the nemesis of Jesus Christ, can only be an image of the condition of their essence; they can vocalize and create pictures of evil since there is no purity within them.

The dragon is unlike the other two who come out of the mouths of physical beings; this would imply that two different armies are present: a human army and a spiritual army. It is why Jesus, with the 144,000, is standing on Mount Zion, awaiting the enemy to advance. He is there to do battle against Satan's army. Satan suffered defeat in Heaven; now, he fights on Earth with his spiritual and physical combatants.

15 "Look, I come like a thief! Blessed is the one who stays awake and remains clothed so as not to go naked and be shamefully exposed."

Here, Jesus is telling us that the one who stays awake and does not go naked, meaning exposed to sin, will be blessed. Those who are clothed must still be present to the end. There is another concealed meaning in this verse: the soldiers' attack with the element of surprise. If you are not wearing the proper clothing or uniform, you will suffer death for being the enemy.

16 "Then they gathered the kings together to the place that in Hebrew is called Armageddon."

John witnesses the armies gathering in the same territory that was once Babylon. The Author continues to focus on this area, where sin originated, for the Drama's conclusion.

17 "The seventh angel poured out his bowl into the air, and out of the temple came a loud voice from the throne, saying, 'It is done!' 18 Then there came flashes of lightning, rumblings, peals of thunder, and a severe earthquake. No earthquake like it has ever occurred since mankind has been on earth, so tremendous was the quake. 19 The great city split into three parts, and the cities of the nations collapsed. God remembered Babylon the Great and gave her the cup filled with the wine of the fury of His wrath. 20 Every Island fled away, and the mountains could not be found. 21 From the sky, huge hailstones, each weighing about a hundred pounds, fell on people. And they cursed God on account of the plague of hail because the plague was so terrible."

Here we have a picture of all the islands disappearing and mountains to be leveled. All cities of the nations were collapsing, beginning with the 'Great City' Jerusalem. Once called the 'Holy City' because God's spirit resided in the Temple, but since the destruction of the Temple, it became the 'Great City.' Jerusalem is Babylon the Great. The ancient nation and city of Babylon collapsed in ancient times. Now, some will say this is the city of Rome. However, this teaching is incorrect and designed to deceive Christians of the truth. Since Rome is called the "Eternal City." The idea of Rome being built on seven hills means nothing. Jerusalem was a city built on seven hills before Rome and called Sodom, Egypt, by God.

Earlier, we discussed the earth speeding up and the world taking on a smaller shape. Here we read that mountains leveled, and every island fled away, resulting in the oceans' shrinking and even disappearing. We will see that God is reshaping the earth for His arrival.

Babylon, the Prostitute on the Beast

Here, we have a chapter that could come before Chapter 16 because one of the Angels with a Bowl will show John what is in store for this Prostitute on a Beast. As in any Drama, physical world, or spirit realm, many events take place simultaneously. Before we start looking into who or what this is, let's forget what we may have learned. Many theologians seem to overlook a great deal of scripture, some prophets regarding the nature and identity of the "Prostitute." She is the nation of Israel. God's prophet Amos records the Lord's saying in 3:2. "You only have I known of all the families of the earth; therefore, I will punish you for all your iniquities." God expects Israel's nation that He is in covenant with to be better than any other country.

This chapter was, so far, one of the more challenging to interpret. However, there is a copious amount of evidence via the scriptures that point to Israel as the Harlot. (the leadership, the government) Much of the commentary I read is very bias and ignores much of the clues throughout scripture altogether. Some theologians enjoy bending scripture. They do this to suit their biased beliefs, which is very dangerous since Revelation comes with a blessing and a curse. I will repeat the Bible from start to finish as a saga between God and His chosen people, the Tribes of Israel, in the setting, an area once known as Babylon.

God has entered into a covenant with Israel provided terms in the Old Covenant, in which Israel vowed, "All that the Lord has said we would do, and be obedient" (Exodus 24:7). Therefore, she had access to God and instruction knowledge, leading to the best physical, mental, and spiritual well-being. God has not entered into any relationship other than the one with Israel. Nevertheless, she has always looked for greener pastures with false gods. Let's continue our journey through Revelation.

(17) "One of the seven angels who had the seven bowls came and said to me, 'Come, I will show you the punishment of the great prostitute, who sits by many waters. 2 With her the kings of the earth committed adultery, and the inhabitants of the earth were intoxicated with the wine of her adulteries.'"

Why is this woman called the 'great prostitute' and 'Babylon the Great'? It must have something to do with Babylon. I am sure God had a reason to identify this woman with Babylon since Babylon was no more at the time of the writing. When used in this context, let's turn to our playbill to define the word "great"; it is not complimentary. The definition of the word in Greek is megas, and it means "big." It can convey suggest something is big or great in size, magnitude, intensity, or rank, in either a good or a bad sense. It depends on the context; this is interesting because when God symbolically dwelt in the Holy of Holies, Jerusalem was known by its citizens as the "Holy City." Since God no longer symbolically lives there, it is no longer 'Holy.'

Tradition tells us, primarily through historian Josephus, that God departed His residence there shortly before AD 70, which led to the Temple's destruction. The "Holy City" title for Jerusalem does not reoccur in God's Drama's conclusion, the book of Revelation, until Revelation 21:2-3. The title "Holy City" reappears in Revelation 21 and is once again applied to Jerusalem, but until that time, when God dwells there, its moniker is 'great city.' However, since God's presence is missing, it is no longer "great" in a moral sense but great, just like Babylon in its anti-God state. Since the presence of God's Holiness is no more, it has become a bad influence and economic, political, and military power. It is not great in holiness. Israel's conduct puts it next to Sodom, Gomorrah, Egypt, and Babylon in great defiance against God. It has abandoned His message and His messengers she has killed, as a result, lost its identification as "the Holy City" and became "great." She is now infamous rather than famous.

We have seen in Revelation 11:8 the identification of Sodom and Egypt, the place of Christ's crucifixion. The moniker of these cities can only apply to Jerusalem. God is giving evidence to identify the nature of the prostitute's character by comparing Israel to Sodom and Egypt. Sodom's reputation in all of the history of mankind for its sexual immorality, and Egypt is known for its harsh and exacting bondage of the Israelite people. A simple example could be, "You're acting just like cousin Babe." If we claim that the Bible is the Word of God, then Jerusalem is the 'great city,' then Jerusalem is the prostitute on the beast. Let us keep in mind that the city symbolizes the nation and its belief in the God of a people no matter where they live.

These two stunning and dramatic comparisons are antecedents of Israel's immoral characteristics in comparison to Babylon. God has already compared Israel to Sodom and Egypt, but there are also two character flaws that God wants to illustrate for Babylon's moniker for Israel: pride and Idol worship. We read that in Exodus the people built an idol to worship before Babylon was a nation.

We read in Ezekiel 16:49, "Look, this was the iniquity of your sister Sodom: She and her daughter had pride, the fullness of food, and abundance of idleness; neither did she strengthen the hand of the poor and needy. (50) And they were haughty and committed abomination before Me; therefore, I took them away as I saw fit. (51) 'Samaria did not commit half of your sins, but you have multiplied your abominations more than they, and have justified your sisters by all the abominations which you have done'".

We notice multiple times that God compares Jerusalem to both Samaria and Sodom and not Rome, or any other city for that matter. God judges Jerusalem; God finds her to be vile and an abomination. These two infamous examples of ancient sinful wickedness are out of control! God portrays these cities as sisters and daughters of the same father, Satan. We all recognize the rebellious behavior of Sodom's sins. God informs us that Samaria had not committed half the crimes that Jerusalem had. These verses put Israel's conduct, not Rome or the Church, by God's judgment and testimony that He calls Israel "Babylon." God provides evidence of the magnitude of Israel's unfaithfulness to her Husband, Benefactor, and God so that we understand the inference of the term "Babylon." God provides a multitude of clues. Therefore, Babylon Harlot on the beast is Jerusalem.

Daniel's stories about Babylon reveal the sin of pride and two significant inadequacies: 1 Babylon has difficulty recognizing God's hand. The visible hand of God in Daniel 5 is symbolic of this. Nebuchadnezzar struggled with the understanding that God was entirely in control of his kingdom. Also, the actives cause events to shape the future, raising and deposing kings and kingdoms. 2 Babylon has difficulty interpreting God's Word. The intellectual wisdom of the entire nation could make no sense of God's simple written word. God's hand wrote four words on the wall of the banquet hall. Babylon thus has trouble interpreting nature and revelation, and the most excellent example of this is Israel in the ability to understand the prophets to recognize Jesus. Daniel's harsh reprimand of Belshazzar's behavior shows that human pride is the cause. God pens the analogy to illustrate that Israel has the exact nature of Babylon.

The effects of the Babylonian captivity on God's people were significant. The most obvious one is the loss of Hebrew as a spoken language. In just two generations, about 70 years, Israel ceased speaking Hebrew and adopted Aramaic, the Babylonian language. It is still expressed in Jesus' day and in the time of the writing of Revelation. Adopting a language is part of assimilating with the culture of the nation. It would include many of the characteristics of the people and their beliefs. Therefore, the Israelites had become like the Babylonians for God to use the moniker "Babylon the Great" or "Babylon the Harlot, " it is not difficult for us to see why. Here we can recall what Jesus said, "Come unto Me, all ye that labor and are heavily laden, and I will give you rest." (Matt 11:28 NIV) God's people have not entirely cast off the burdens of a Babylonian lifestyle, so Israel still speaks, eats, and breathes Babylonian.

Israel became prosperous while in Babylon, even becoming part of the ruling class as Joseph had done in Egypt. The Israelites were permitted to live freely and maintain their religious beliefs. However, since the destruction of Solomon's Temple, the people of Israel living in Babylon could no longer practice their faith as God had ordered them to do. It caused them to make social adjustments. The Babylonian Talmud was a development by the priestly class. The Babylonian Talmud was used during Christ's day and was edited around 500 AD and is still used and referred to by the same name.

The Talmud is the only religious document still used today with the name Babylon in its title. It is a collection of thoughts written by Jewish Rabbis. Therefore it is not the Word of God. Since this is a collection of ideas coming forth from Babylon and used during the writing of Revelation, it is with us today. It is safe to assume that it is another piece of evidence pointing to today's Israel and Jerusalem as the prostitute on the beast. The Babylonian Talmud claims that Jesus is the son of a prostitute and that He is in Hell. I find it interesting that the title of the book Babylon Talmud is a Jewish religious book. Zionist-inspired Christian false Theologians would have you think that the Roman Catholic Church is Babylon when God's Word says otherwise, while the Roman Catholic Church reads from the Bible God's Word at every Mass.

None of these three terms, Sodom, Egypt, or Babylon, are an attractive comparison. Every one of them illustrates how God sees Jerusalem and Israel. God points out that Israel and Jerusalem's pride has blinded them from understanding that they are on the same spiritual and moral level as Sodom, Egypt, and Babylon. God provides His harshest judgments on some, "Because the Lord disciplines the one he loves, and he chastens everyone he accepts as His Son" (Hebrews 12:6). He does this, especially for those who should know better but waste their gifts in prideful self-indulgence.

Here, we have another clue of many waters. A place with several rivers and streams, but the symbolic meaning may be of different nations and people of various tongues. The next is with her; the kings of the earth committed adultery. Let's ask ourselves a simple question: which is more likely for a king to desire based on every king mentioned in the Bible? Wealth or Religion? King Solomon makes this request from God, "Give me wisdom and knowledge, that I may lead this people, for who is able to govern this great people of yours?" (2 Chronicles 1:10) God responds to King Solomon, "God said to Solomon, 'Because you had this in mind, and did not ask for riches, wealth or honor, or the life of those who hate you, nor have you even asked for long life, but you have asked for yourself wisdom and knowledge that you may rule My people over whom I have made you king, 12 wisdom and knowledge have been granted to you." There seems to be a bit of irony here since, in the end, Solomon turns out to be rather foolish and not wise at all since he builds temples for the gods of his many wives.

Therefore, it is safe to assume that Kings always seek wealth. A modern-day example is today's politicians who enter public office working with a salary and somehow manage to have a net worth of 150 million or more. Did they seek to do the will of God, serve the people, or line their pockets? It is an example of those in a principal office in Washington, DC that has acquired wealth at the expense of the people they serve, and other leaders of other nations are no different. Who was it that helped them behind the scenes but the Harlot? So, the wine of her adultery is the desire for wealth, the idol of gold and silver, and sexual immorality.

We see this behavior all through the Book of Judges. "For the love of money is a root of all kinds of evil." Some people, eager for money, have wandered from the faith and pierced themselves with many griefs." (1 Timothy 6:10 NIV) However, false teachers would have you think it was a false religion that corrupted the kings. Here is what God had to say, "And I saw that for all the adulteries of faithless Israel, I had sent her away and given her a writ of divorce, yet her treacherous sister Judah did not fear; but she went and was a harlot also. 9 Because of the lightness of her harlotry, she polluted the land and committed adultery with stones and trees. 10 Yet in spite of all this, her treacherous sister Judah did not return to Me with all her heart, but rather in deception," declares the Lord." (Jeremiah 3: 8-9 NIV)

Here is another example of who God says is the Harlot from Ezekiel 16:27-30. "Behold; therefore, I stretched out My hand against you, diminished your allotment, and gave you up to the will of those who hate you, the daughters of the Philistines, who were ashamed of your lewd behavior. You also played the harlot with the Assyrians because you were insatiable; indeed, you played the harlot with them, and still, you were not satisfied. Moreover, you multiplied your acts of harlotry as far as the trader's land, Chaldea, and even then, you were not satisfied. How degenerate is your heart," says the Lord God, "seeing you do all these things, the deeds of a brazen harlot."

During Christ's time on earth, the Pharisees often did favors for the Romans to stay in power and earn wealth. Shakespeare, in The Merchant of Venice, has a Jewish character Shylock lends money to the Duke. Today, members of the Jewish community own all of the Federal Government banks of the world. We see it during Christ's time; Shakespeare presents it in his time, and we can see it in our time. Since the Federal Reserve Bank owners in the USA can print money, it doesn't have and lends it to the government with interest. The same group owns all of the government banks in the world. The owners are Ashkenazi Jews; the same group owns the media centers as well. This fact alone would strongly imply that Israel fornicated with the Kings of the world. "For the Lord, your God will bless you as he has promised, and you will lend to many nations but will borrow from none." (Deuteronomy 15:6 NIV) We follow the action as the scene changes out to the wilderness with John.

3 "Then the angel carried me away in the Spirit into a wilderness. There, I saw a woman sitting on a scarlet beast that was covered with blasphemous names and had seven heads and ten horns. 4 The woman was dressed in purple and scarlet and was glittering with gold, precious stones, and pearls. She held a golden cup in her hand, filled with abominable things and the filth of her adulteries. 5 The name written on her forehead was a mystery, "Babylon the Great," the mother of prostitutes and of the abominations of the earth."

We pause the scene to notice that elegant clothing, jewelry, and precious metals or gold and silver illustrate her wealth. It is a wealth of the hoarding of things. It is the outward sign of pride to display success. As a group, the Israelite people, the descendants of Abraham, Isaac, and Jacob, grew to control around 60% of the world's wealth at the height of their prosperity. Today, Rothschild, another Jewish family, possesses over 50% of the world's wealth, a net worth of 500 trillion dollars. They could pay the debt of the world and still be the richest family. Jacob Rothschild claims himself to be the 21st-century King of the Jews. It would seem very likely that his heir would be their 'Messiah'; the one who will rule the world is the Zionist dream.

When we take a good look, we find that the tribes of Jacob have corrupted and destroyed every nation where they have lived. First, Joseph put the Egyptians in slavery when they did not have enough food while making his family wealthy; later, the tables turned, and became slaves. Next, they invited the Muslims into Spain during the Ottoman Empire. Then, look at what they are doing to Europe. First, the streets are lined with Muslims living on the sidewalks of Paris, and now America is being invaded by Islam due to wealthy Nazi Soros.

Today, as in the past, the Israelites are in the position to influence, persuade, and guide humanity in the media, universities, and government through the misuse of gifts God has given them. Israel has fallen like Satan to worldly greatness and spiritual immortality, considerable in its confusion, extensive in its deviance from responsibility, and immense in its polluting influence of evil. We see this demonstration throughout the film industry, producing pornographic films that display all forms of sexual immorality. Like the Koran, the Talmud permits sexual activity with children.

Only Israel, the Harlot, the Bribe of the Dragon, is so dominant in its power that she can hold the Beast in check. She makes it do her bidding until Jesus Christ returns. Throughout the Saga of God's Drama, no other nation is a cheating, dishonest wife who takes up with other lovers. The Bible is also a Love Story between a kind, loving man and a prostitute, as portrayed in Hosea 1:2. "When the Lord began to speak through Hosea, the Lord said to him, 'Go, marry a promiscuous woman and have children with her, for like an adulterous wife this land is guilty of unfaithfulness to the Lord.'" The book of Hosea is, in many ways, a summary of God's relationship with Israel. Let's return to the scene with John.

6 "I saw that the woman was drunk with the blood of God's holy people, the blood of those who bore testimony to Jesus. When I saw her, I was greatly astonished. 7 Then the angel said to me: 'Why are you astonished? I will explain to you the mystery of the woman and of the beast she rides, which has seven heads and ten horns. 8 The beast, which you saw, once was, now is not, and yet will come up out of the Abyss and go to its destruction. The inhabitants of the earth whose names have not been written in the book of life from the creation of the world will be astonished when they see the beast because it once was, now is not, and yet will come.'"

God, the Drama Author we call the Bible, uses repetition to reinforce certain characters, characteristics, and events. I spent days meditating and time in prayer before commenting on these three verses. Once again, it can only refer to Israel, the nation, its people, and Jerusalem. Scripture tells us that Jerusalem killed the prophets. Christ died in Jerusalem by the religious leaders, and those who practiced the Hebrew Faith also murdered Christ's followers. Therefore, she represents the leaders of the Jews Faith. It is they who have become drunk with blood. She rides a beast, the kingdom of Judah/Israel, with its capital on seven Jerusalem hills.

More than 14 major cities were built on seven hills: Babylon, Istanbul, Mecca, Rome, and Jerusalem, to name a few, with Babylon and Jerusalem being established long before the others. Mecca and Istanbul are both in the territory that was once part of the Babylonian nation. The beast comes forth out of the Abyss. We have already seen the release of a fallen angel,

Abaddon, from his imprisonment in the Abyss. John is astonished to see Israel's nation restored after coming out of a place of evil, the Second World War. Israel was a nation that once was and is no more at the time of the writing. It came out of the Abyss, and it is now a nation. Thanks to President Donald J. Trump, Jerusalem is now the recognized capital of Israel.

9 "This calls for a mind with wisdom. The seven heads are seven hills on which the woman sits. 10 They are also seven kings. Five have fallen; one is, the other has not yet come, but when he does come, he must remain for only a little while. 11 The beast who once was, and now is not, is an eighth king. He belongs to the seven and is going to his destruction."

The symbolic woman is Jerusalem, and she sits on the seven hills of Jerusalem. The meaning of the five kings and kingdoms that have fallen before John's writing revelation are Israel, Babylon, Median, Persian, and Greece. Rome is the one that followed for a little while in the Ottoman Empire/Arab Kingdom. The eighth is the return of Israel, which was part of the seven empires. Egypt is left out here because it did not occupy any of the territories of Babylon. Thus, Egypt was a powerful nation before Israel was a nation with a Kingdom.

The angel continues to explain as we watch John listen to what he says.

12 "The ten horns you saw are ten kings who have not yet received a kingdom, but who for one hour will receive authority as kings along with the beast. 13 They have one purpose and will give their power and

authority to the beast. 14 They will wage war against the Lamb, but the Lamb will triumph over them because He is Lord of lords and King of kings—and with Him will be his called, chosen and faithful followers."

The meaning behind these verses is once the Harlot returns, meaning the Nation of Israel as a Kingdom, a government that will seek global rule. The beast, the false messiah, will give ten minor kings the authority to support the creature. They will wage war against Christians, and that war has begun, but the Lamb, the true King, will triumph over them. Here is another deception by Zionist Christians. Theologians suggest the Catholic Church is the Harlot. It will wage war against itself when we have two religions that have opposed Christianity for centuries, the Jewish faith since Christ and Islam since the seventh century. These two groups have taken two different approaches to destroy Christianity: Islam through extermination and Jewry through financial slavery and moral corruption. I find it interesting that 1.2 percent of abortions are conducted by Jewish women, while more than 80 percent are Christian women. The credit for the Supreme Court ruling goes to a Jewish female judge.

With a bit of research, you can find ten nations dangerous for Christians: North Korea, Somalia, Sudan, Eritrea, Nigeria, Libya, Vietnam, Central African Republic, Kenya, Ethiopia, and Egypt. For example, Obama with his possibly birth in Kenya, but even without it, Obama has a family there, and you can recall how he spoke negatively about Christians and Jesus. There are many more dangerous places for Christians.

15 "Then the angel said to me, 'The waters you saw, where the prostitute sits, are peoples, multitudes, nations, and languages. 16 The beast and the ten horns you saw will hate the prostitute. They will bring her to ruin and leave her naked; they will eat her flesh and burn her with fire. 17 For God has put it into their hearts to accomplish his purpose by agreeing to hand over to the beast their royal authority, until God's words are fulfilled. 18 The woman you saw is the great city that rules over the kings of the earth.'"

The harlot represents the nation of Israel and mainly the city of Jerusalem. The beast is the political power ruled as a "King" with a somewhat diverse and competing application of the Mosaic Law, similar to the Babylonian system. The Beast of the Sea is the individual representing the harlot. The Sea Beast is her voice, which is the voice of the Dragon. The Beast of the Earth would be her prophet, who glorifies the beast of the sea; this is a mirror image of Exodus 7:1: "Then the Lord said to Moses, 'See, I have made you like God to Pharaoh, and your brother Aaron will be your prophet.'" These two men were Levites who governed Israel before a king, while the beast with seven heads represents Judah, the line of kings.

A rivalry is present within the Jewish community between the Torah-practicing Jews and the Zionists. The competition, according to this principle in Mark 3:24-26, will eventually escalate into war. This division has already taken place within Israeli government policy. Each group desires world domination and the enslavement of the gentile races. Today, the media divides various gentile groups, blacks against whites, and Muslims against Christians. Like the serpent in the garden, they encourage and even pay for the division to conquer. Jesus stated that Satan's divided house could not stand the Babylonian system that failed to hold once before, failing to stay again. Here, we have another clue as to why Rome is neither the harlot nor the beast. Rome developed a system of government that of a republic. Today Islam resembles an ancient form of governing in their Sharia Law. It would make Istanbul, a city on seven hills in Turkey, better for this character than Rome. However, neither group has had the number of covenants between them and God that Israel shares. Therefore, they cannot break a contract they never had.

We see how the competition between these two will go. Revelation 17 begins with the woman is comfortably sitting and riding on the beast. But by the end, the woman has been thrown off and gobbled up by the beast. Next, it will occur when God hardens the hearts of the kings. God's intervention for the woman has managed to keep the community together while in the diaspora. She may seem weaker than this wild beast, but the faith leaders were actually in control much of the time. Finally, however, God will permit the beast to destroy the harlot. The harlot is the religious system of Israel and the leaders of the faith. Keep in mind that Israel has rejected the Son of God, not the Roman Catholic Church.

Lament Over Fallen Babylon

After a brief intermission, we are back to view what John sees next.

18 "After this, I saw another angel coming down from Heaven. He had great authority, and the earth was illuminated by his splendor. 2 With a mighty voice he shouted: 'Fallen! Fallen is Babylon the Great! She has become a dwelling for demons and a haunt for every impure spirit, a haunt for every unclean bird, and a haunt for every unclean and detestable animal. 3 For all the nations have drunk the maddening wine of her adulteries. The kings of the earth committed adultery with her, and the merchants of the earth grew rich from her excessive luxuries.'"

We have already reviewed the notion that kings have little care about religion. King Henry VIII started the Angelo Church to give himself a divorce since the Roman Church refused him. "Babylon the Great" refers to a nation and an economic nerve center of world trade and not religion. What most theologians fail to realize is that the concept of a nation. We prefer to think of a country with borders and people within the boundaries of the same culture. The same theologians will refer to the Roman Catholic Church, which has a Vatican City location, but its people are scattered all over the earth. They speak a different language, are citizens of other nations, and are also the offspring of different countries. Ironically, so are those of the Jewish Faith. They have their religious centers and synagogues in various nations. They speak the language of the societies where they live. The difference, however, is that for nearly two thousand years, they were a nation without borders.

To preserve their nation of Israel and their identity as a people, they only pretended to assimilate. Unlike the Diaspora in Babylon, where they assimilated through their synagogues, they maintained their traditions and laws as people in the hope of returning to their homeland someday. In the meantime, like their ancestor, Joseph, they became wealthy and even held positions of power within the nations where they lived.

Today, they control all the world's finances: the media, the universities, the publishing houses, and many other industries that influence the minds of the gentiles. They have provided funds for kings, and today, they even fund presidential campaigns. Members of the Jewish community have held political office. "The Lord will open the heavens, the storehouse of his bounty, to send rain on your land in season and to bless all the work of your hands. You will lend too many nations but will borrow from none." (Deuteronomy 28:12 NIV) God, as kept his promise to them.

Hence, first, the kings of the earth grieve her destruction, and then the businessmen follow suit because she has made them rich. Only those with a biased hatred for the Roman Church would want you to imagine both the kings of the earth and hardheaded people in business lamenting over the destruction of a church! These leaders are weeping for the removal of a deceitful lover they have fornicated to gain power and wealth. They also mourn for themselves for their guilt and involvement with the Harlot. They now realize her destruction places them in grave danger of overwhelming loss because Babylon can no longer provide for their wealth.

When we close a book, the back cover reflects the front cover. In a well-written essay, the last paragraph restates the opening with a conclusion. So it is with "God's Historical Novel," the ending reflects the beginning with the conflict's resolution. God, the Master of all authors, provides clues for us with these simple reading and writing techniques. Joseph, an Israelite, becomes Governor and is in charge of Pharaoh's wealth in Egypt's land. No one could buy food without Joseph's orders. People hail Joseph for his remarks about saving lives, but they forget to mention that the government-owned everything by the end of the seven-year famine in Egypt. Joseph forced people to sell everything they owned to eat. In the end, he put people into slavery, but not his father and brothers and their families. In the final episode of God's saga, the last Joseph will be the beast of the earth, representing Pharaoh, the beast of the sea, in the land of "Egypt," the Harlot of Israel.

Now we hear a "Warning to Escape Babylon's Judgment"

4 "Then I heard another voice from heaven say: Come out of her, my people, so that you will not share

in her sins, so that you will not receive any of her plagues; 5 for her sins are piled up to heaven, and God has remembered her crimes. 6 Give back to her as she has given; pay her back double for what she has done. Pour her a double portion from her own cup 7 Give her as much torment and grief as the glory and luxury she gave herself. In her heart she boasts, 'I sit enthroned as queen. I am not a widow; I will never mourn.' 8 Therefore in one day her plagues will overtake her: death, mourning, and famine. She will be consumed by fire, for mighty is the Lord God who judges her."

These verses could easily apply to America, and we do have a queen standing in a harbor. The Zionists are destroying the foundation of America's original system by corrupting the morals of Americans. God has a similar plan for Babylon the Great. God will terminate her the way he did Egypt; the irony is that the nation that received salvation will receive her final punishment. God calls out, come out of her, My people. God gives the sons and daughters living in Sodom/Egypt/Jerusalem to come up and leave for salvation. The difference here is that to come out, one needs the seal of Christ and His Salvation. I wish to repeat it here again: God, through the scripture, does not give Rome the moniker of Sodom or Egypt. He has, however, delivered to Jerusalem, a city in the nation of Israel that killed the prophets and Christ. Rome was never the Bride of God. All Christians together form the Bride of Christ.

Throughout the entire Biblical Saga, only the offspring of the 12 tribes of Israel are God's people. However, through Faith, others are graphed into the family of

God. When God says, My people, He is inferring to Israel's offspring, the 12 tribes, and their offspring. When we read the Book of Exodus and study it carefully, we conclude that God has destroyed Egypt's economic structure with the plagues. God terminates all plant and animal goods, reduces their firstborn workforce, and finally eliminates their military power. We also discover that the Hebrews, Israelites, and their livestock while living in Goshen are untouched by the plagues. In the final episode, God pours His wrath on those with the mark of the beast, not those who have the Christ seal.

There is another fascinating clue that appears in Genesis and Exodus, which surfaces here and his firstborn. From the beginning, the firstborn right goes to a younger brother. Cain kills Abel, and Seth replaces him. Ishmael, the firstborn but second-born Isaac, is the son of promise. Next is Esau, who sells his birthright to Jacob. Judah replaces Reuben. God, the Author of the drama, must have a reason to keep exchanging the firstborn with the next in line. We also can observe that the firstborn, in the same manner, falls short of God's requirement. Both Cain and Reuben comment on an act of violence. Esau sells his birthright for a bowl of stew, and the nation of Israel/Judah, the firstborn as a nation, rejects the firstborn Son of God by having Jesus crucified and replaced by the children of faith, the younger brother, also referred to as the church. Like both Ishmael and Esau, Israel's nation thinks she is entitled because she was first, but she broke her covenant with God more than once and will do so again.

God, the Master Writer, presents us with three significant characteristics of Babylon. She glorified herself; she lived extravagantly, and she proclaimed herself a queen and not a widow who would see any sorrow. God is painting with words an end-time city/nation that is exceedingly wealthy and influential. As a result, she is disdainful, contemptuous, and mocking. One needs only to read the Talmud to see what the Harlot thinks of Jesus Christ. God's verbal portrayal is that she is proud to the point of arrogance and self-confidence, believing she has produced power and security by her means. She lives extravagantly compared to other nations' levels while simultaneously compromising moral standards to gratify her sinful lust.

A city of lust could also be a picture of Los Angeles or even New York before the Vatican, what we have by way of a national symbol for a nation of people who are arrogant, prideful satiety, super-abundance of money and material things, and avoidance of suffering, a compromising, self-absorbed, self-indulgence. These are also the characteristics of the people of this culture. We can find this attitude in the plutocracy. These elites are incredibly wealthy Zionists who own and control most of the world's wealth, and Jerusalem is a great city. It is Israel's sentiment, "To be a real Israeli, you must be Jewish." Also, a "real Israeli" must speak Hebrew. My guess is the same people would say the statement to be American, you must be a Christian and speak English is racist.

Threefold Woe Over Babylon's Fall

Let's return to John and the written Word of God.

9 "When the kings of the earth who committed adultery with her and shared her luxury see the smoke of her burning, they will weep and mourn over her. 10 Terrified at her torment, they will stand far off and cry: Woe! Woe to you, great city, you mighty city of Babylon! 'In one hour your doom has come!'"

11 "The merchants of the earth will weep and mourn over her because no one buys their cargoes anymore 12 cargoes of gold, silver, precious stones, and pearls; fine linen, purple, silk and scarlet cloth; every sort of citron wood, and articles of every kind made of ivory, costly wood, bronze, iron, and marble; 13 cargoes of cinnamon and spice, of incense, myrrh, and frankincense, of wine and olive oil, of fine flour and wheat; cattle and sheep; horses and carriages; and human beings sold as slaves."

Contrary to many of the theologians who use the Heidelberg Catechism, Revelation 17 and 18 do not describe a church. It represents a city/nation involved in the global control of massive worldwide merchandising and manufacturing. Let us face the truth: it was Jewish merchants who commercialized Christmas to earn money from the Christians. These organizations want to eliminate the words Merry Christmas to Happy Holidays and slowly remove any connection to Jesus Christ. They have organizations such as the Anti-Defamation League (ADL), the American Civil Liberties Union (ACLU), the Southern Poverty Law Center (SPLC), the American Jewish Committee (AJC), and many others. They have bought, bribed, threatened, or otherwise manipulated our Congress, Senate, and Presidency. It is an attempt to eliminate Christianity from America. Liberals in California want to ban the

Bible. America would be more likely the Harlot of Babylon than the Roman Catholic Church.
Today, a stock market exchange is an example of selling these goods, just mentioned in verses 11-13, from a single place. The broad stock markets are New York, London, and Tel Aviv Stock Exchange; so do the others when one falls. Only in the imagination of some biased theologians would anyone dream of describing a church organization trading and selling commodities and shares in corporations. Since the Roman Catholic Church has never engaged in manufacturing, nor has it been the actual seller of manufactured goods. Hence, the only possible solution is a city/state as "Babylon the Great." Revelation 17 provides no evidence directly tying the woman riding the Beast to a religion. Thus far, there is not any shred of evidence linking Babylon in any form to Rome. New York City would be a better guess since Wall Street houses the world's leading stock exchange.
Let's continue with this Chapter.

14 "They will say, 'The fruit you longed for is gone from you. All your luxury and splendor have vanished, never to be recovered.' 15 The merchants who sold these things and gained their wealth from her will stand far off, terrified at her torment. They will weep and mourn 16 and cry out: 'Woe! Woe to you, great city, dressed in fine linen, purple and scarlet, and glittering with gold, precious stones, and pearls 17 In one hour, such great wealth has been brought to ruin!'"
"Every sea captain, and all who travel by ship, the sailors, and all who earn their living from the sea, will stand far off. 18 When they see the smoke of her burning, they will exclaim, 'Was there ever a city like this great city?' 19 They will throw dust on their heads

and, with weeping and mourning, cry out: Woe! Woe to you, great city, where all who had ships on the sea became rich through her wealth! In one hour, she has been brought to ruin! 20 Rejoice over her, you heavens! Rejoice, you people of God! Rejoice, apostles and prophets! For God has judged her with the judgment she imposed on you."

We have three outstanding clues. One is that a church does not operate in a seaport. The second is that Israel/Judah is responsible for killing the prophets and the apostles. The term Babylon is just another moniker that God uses to describe the nature of Israel. The last one is in one hour she is brought to ruin. A stock market crash in one hour could bankrupt every nation and its people. One more outstanding fact that everyone overlooks is that it is so simple. I laughed when the Still Small Voice spoke and said, "After all the plagues, the wealthy are dead. They did not have the seal of Christ, and many will be Jewish." One Jewish family alone controls 50% of the world's wealth now put them all together, and if they die, indeed, the merchants of the earth will be crying. Theologians avoid this detail; 'seaport' could reference New York, but Israel has three significant seaports: the Port of Haifa, the Port of Ashdod, and the Port of Eilat. And they all serve passenger and merchant ships, once again, in the earlier territory of Babylon. Oh! Rome does not have a seaport. Yes, Italy does.

The Finality of Babylon's Doom

21 "Then a mighty angel picked up a boulder the size of a large millstone and threw it into the sea, and said: 'With such violence the great city of Babylon will be

thrown down, never to be found again.' 22 The music of harpists and musicians, pipers and trumpeters, will never be heard in you again. No worker of any trade will ever be found in you again. The sound of a millstone will never be heard in you again."

23 "The light of a lamp will never shine in you again. The voice of bridegroom and bride will never be heard in you again. Your merchants were the world's important people. By your magic spell, all the nations were led astray. 24 In her was found the blood of prophets and of God's holy people, of all who have been slaughtered on the earth."

Some might claim that the Catholic Church has killed people, which is true, but the Angelic Church of England has done the same. Christians of all denominations have killed people, but they did not destroy God's prophets, nor did they kill Jesus Christ. Jewish people will argue that the Romans killed Jesus, but they refuse to accept that they first denied Jesus, then protested and requested that the Romans kill him since the Roman law forbids them to do it. Pilate washed his hands, ordered them to choose, and they demanded a murderer go free and crucify Christ, claiming that now Christ's blood was not on their hands since the Romans performed the act, but God knows different.

Threefold Hallelujah Over Babylon's Fall

Now the scene totally changes to Heaven where John hears cheers.

19 "After this, I heard what sounded like the roar of a great multitude in heaven shouting: 'Hallelujah! Salvation and glory and power belong to our God, 2 for true and just are his judgments. He has condemned the great prostitute who corrupted the earth by her adulteries. He has avenged on her the blood of His servants.' 3 And again they shouted: 'Hallelujah!' The smoke from her goes up forever and ever. 4 The twenty-four elders and the four living creatures fell down and worshiped God, who was seated on the throne. And they cried: Amen, Hallelujah!"

We hear the redeemed voices and those from under the altar who have waited for this moment. (Rev. 6:9: NIV) These redeemed souls are cheering as a choir and giving praise to the Lord Jesus Christ. The reclaimed have been looking on from heaven and are approving of the destruction of Babylon the Great. Christ has brought justice and righteousness to the world. The many martyred have waited a long time for God's judgment. John hears a voice coming from the throne.

5 "Then a voice came from the throne, saying: 'Praise our God, all you His servants, you who fear Him, both great and small!' 6 Then I heard what sounded like a great multitude, like the roar of rushing waters and like loud peals of thunder, shouting: Hallelujah! For our Lord God Almighty reigns. 7 Let us rejoice and be glad and give Him glory! For the wedding of the Lamb has come, and his bride has made herself ready. 8 Fine linen, bright and clean, was given her to wear." (Fine linen stands for the righteous acts of God's holy people.)

The Lamb's marriage as come does not mean the actual feast, but the final preparations are underway. The Lamb still has a significant battle to finish before the actual wedding day. The bribe of Christ is not Israel but the Church, the believers. God has already divorced from Israel. Understand that killing Jesus Christ was also killing God; therefore, how can she continue to be His Bribe?

This marriage is the eternal union between the Church and Christ following the Harvest. The fine linen, clean, and white wedding gown represents the righteousness of the Church, which has now been judged and purified at the judgment seat of Christ (1 Cor. 3:12-15: 2 Cor. 5:10) Judgment Seat of Christ. This wedding ceremony replaces the one between God and Israel and becomes one between God and all believers.

In ancient times, the single most fabulous celebration and social event was the marriage between a man and a woman. The occasion came in three distinct stages. The first involved the betrothal or engagement. The arrangement took part by both sets of parents and was legally binding and could only end in divorce. It is followed by a time of preparation as the groom prepares a place for his bride. Next was the presentation, which was a time of festivities before the actual ceremony. The celebrations could last up to a week or more, depending on the bride and groom's economic or social status. Finally, the festivities conclude with the wedding ceremony with the exchanging of vows. This same wedding planning is part of the Lord's relationship with His Church.

Now, an angel is about to speak to John. 9 "Then the angel said to me, 'Write this: Blessed are those who are invited to the wedding supper of the Lamb!' And he added, 'These are the true words of God.' 10 At this, I fell at his feet to worship him. But he said to me, 'Don't do that! I am a fellow servant with you and with your brothers and sisters who hold to the testimony of Jesus. Worship God! For it is the Spirit of prophecy who bears testimony to Jesus.'"

It is pretty self-exclamatory. You are blessed if you are part of the ceremony, and that the whole Biblical Story is about Jesus and the salvation of the world. The offspring would crush the head of the serpent. We come full circle to witness the fulfillment of that event, and now for the final conflict with the nemesis, the dragon. We watch with John as Jesus rides out for the final battle.

The Heavenly Warrior Defeats the Beast

11 "I saw heaven standing open and there before me was a white horse, whose rider is called Faithful and

True. With justice, he judges and wages war. 12 His eyes are like blazing fire, and on his head are many crowns. He has a name written on him that no one knows but He himself. 13 He is dressed in a robe dipped in blood, and his name is the Word of God. 14 The armies of heaven were following him, riding on white horses and dressed in fine linen, white and clean. 15 Coming out of his mouth is a sharp sword with which to strike down the nations. 'He will rule them with an iron scepter.' He treads the winepress of the fury of the wrath of God Almighty 16 On his robe and on his thigh he has this name written: King of kings and Lord of lords."

There is a formal introduction of the Lord of lords, the one and only Son of God, Jesus Christ. I don't believe He needs an army behind Him. They would be following Christ as a witness to the event. Christ could stand alone on the battlefield and defeat His enemies with just a Word, and we shall see that He does. I often picture Jesus as a mighty warrior who could stand before the greatest of Kung Fu Masters and kill with just thought because He holds the keys to both life and death; this is the meaning of out of His mouth comes to a two-edged sword. His Word can give life or death. Let us return to the scene of the action on our stage.

17 And I saw an angel standing in the sun, who cried in a loud voice to all the birds flying in midair, "Come, gather together for the great supper of God, 18 so that you may eat the flesh of kings, generals, and the mighty, of horses and their riders, and the flesh of all people, free and slave, great and small."

It seems that this is a very literal statement that does not need much interpretation that God is having birds eat the flesh of these followers of the evil trio, the dragon, the sea beast, and the earth beast, right where they died. This is very similar to 2 Kings 6:17-18: "17 And Elisha prayed, 'Open his eyes, Lord, so that he may see.' Then the Lord opened the servant's eyes, and he looked and saw the hills full of horses and chariots of fire all around Elisha. 18 As the enemy came down toward him, Elisha prayed to the Lord, "Strike this army with blindness." So he struck them with blindness, as Elisha had asked." The difference here is that the evil army dies and becomes food for the birds.

19 "Then I saw the beast and the kings of the earth and their armies gathered together to wage war against the rider on the horse and his army. 20 But the beast was captured and with it the false prophet who had performed the signs on its behalf. With these signs, he had deluded those who had received the mark of the beast and worshiped its image. The two of them were thrown alive into the fiery lake of burning sulfur. 21 The rest were killed with the sword coming out of the mouth of the rider on the horse, and all the birds gorged themselves on their flesh."

We have a fascinating comment here, and it is the first time in the book of Revelation that anyone leaves earth while still being alive. The beast and the false prophet are thrown alive into the fiery lake of burning sulfur. Here, we mention two evil beings going to the lake of fire still alive in body form; why doesn't Revelation use the words alive into Heaven? If the rapture is an actual event, why isn't it stated as plainly as these two going into the lake of fire alive? The answer is simple because God did not order it, and nor is it written. There is one other clue. Those who are raisin from the dead and found guilty go into the lake of fire in bodily form.

Since the three demon frog creatures go and assemble an army, who are they going to fight? If the so-called rapture took place, then there cannot be a good army of Christian believers. Next, with all of the plagues, a large number of people have already died. The possibility of new believers having the ability to come together as an army with little or no weapons seems unlikely. The current plan is to remove guns from honest Christian citizens. Therefore, the dragon's followers and the beasts can see Jesus Christ and His army coming against them. It is a clear example of demonic insanity. How can an army made of men with physical bodies that die think that they can defeat an army of beings who cannot perish because they are immortal beings?

The dragon knows that his human army will die because he plans to destroy humankind. The dragon and his demons wish to destroy Christ to re-enter Heaven, but they are defeated and cast into prison for a thousand years, in my fictional tale titled An Interview with Death. I present Satan as dumb and clueless. His jealousy and lust for power have clouded his mind. As a result, he destroys himself, much like many leaders and celebrities of today.

Thousand Years

Now begins the Glorious Reign of JESUS CHRIST.

(20) "And I saw an angel coming down out of Heaven, having the key to the Abyss and holding in his hand a great chain. 2 He seized the dragon, that ancient serpent, who is the devil, or Satan, and bound him for a thousand years. 3 He threw him into the Abyss and locked and sealed it over him to keep him from deceiving the nations anymore until the thousand years were ended. After that, he must be set free for a short time."

In the Book of Enoch, God sends Raphael to bind Azazel, aka Abaddon, in the bottom of the Abyss and then covers him with rocks so he cannot see any light. He is set free from the Abyss as the King of the locust. After the sound of one of the Trumpets, now we have an angel holding in his hand a chain to bind the dragon in the same Abyss for a thousand years, and as Abaddon, he will be sent free for a short time before casting him into the lake of fire. Jude 6 confirms the Book of Enoch. "And the angels who did not keep their positions of authority, but abandoned their proper dwelling these God has kept in darkness, bound with everlasting chains for judgment on the Great Day." We return to the stage to witness what John sees next.

4 "I saw thrones on which were seated those who had been given authority to judge. And I saw the souls of those who had been beheaded because of their testimony about Jesus and because of the Word of God. They had not worshiped the beast or its image and had not received its mark on their foreheads or their hands. They came to life and reigned with Christ for a thousand years. 5 The rest of the dead did not come to life until the thousand years were ended. This is the first resurrection. 6 Blessed and holy are those who share in the first resurrection. The second death has no power over them, but they will be priests of God and of Christ and will reign with him for a thousand years."

What John witnesses are the martyrs who died for Christ. The group is all the martyrs who have held fast to the end without renouncing Christ. The only other group that will be present are still physically alive after all of the plagues and wars. Once again, there is no mention of raptured believers up to this point.

The Judgment of Satan

7 "When the thousand years are over, Satan will be released from his prison 8 and will go out to deceive the nations in the four corners of the earth Gog and Magog and to gather them for battle. In number, they are like the sand on the seashore. 9 They marched across the breadth of the earth and surrounded the camp of God's people, the city he loves. But fire came down from heaven and devoured them. 10 And the devil, who deceived them, was thrown into the lake of burning sulfur, where the beast and the false prophet

had been thrown. They will be tormented day and night forever and ever."

Now, Satan has been imprisoned like Abaddon and does not change or repent. He again tries to take the Kingdom away from Christ. He is using those who are of Gog and Magog. It would seem that the members of these two groups are those who never died and survived the plagues. They had repented, but as the Israelites of Exodus and Judges quickly return to their old ways, this is a group that Satan the Dragon influences once again because, in their hearts, they do not wish to praise God and Christ. Perhaps they, like Satan, are jealous and envious that others have a higher standing position as Priests or Judges in this Millennium. Therefore, with the promise of more senior status and wealth, they join in the rebellion that the Lord squashes quickly, sending the uprising and their leader into the burning lake of fire.

The Judgment of the Dead

11 "Then I saw a great white throne and him who was seated on it. The earth and the heavens fled from his presence, and there was no place for them. 12 And I saw the dead, great and small, standing before the throne, and books were opened. Another book was opened, which is the Book of Life. The dead were judged according to what they had done as recorded in the books. 13 The sea gave up the dead that were in it, and death and Hades gave up the dead that were in them, and each person was judged according to what they had done. 14 Then death and Hades were thrown into the lake of fire. The lake of fire is the second death. 15 Anyone whose name was not found

written in the Book of Life was thrown into the lake of fire."

Now, everyone who has ever died is resurrected from the dead. John sees the names of those not in the Book of Life cast into the lake of fire without any need for further judgment. Next are those who are in the Book of Life. Now, the other book deals with what you have done with your faith in God and Christ. "Whatever you do, work at it with all your heart, as working for the Lord, not for human masters, since you know that you will receive an inheritance from the Lord as a reward. It is the Lord Christ you are serving." (Colossians 3:23-24 NIV)

It is also written, "God will repay each person according to what they have done." (Romans 2:6 NIV) There are other passages in scripture that would support the notion of Heavenly rewards for the works of one's heart. James had this to say; "In the same way, was not even Rahab the prostitute considered righteous for what she did when she gave lodging to the spies and sent them off in a different direction? 26 As the body without the spirit is dead, so faith without deeds is dead." (James 2:25-26 NIV) Therefore, this other Book is a record of our faith's fruit, and as a result, comes various rewards. Finally, the Sermon on the Mount is another clue of what those rewards may be in Matthew 5 - 7.

A New Heaven and a New Earth

We have come to the end of the Drama, an end to our Journey. We can only wonder concerning the excitement and joy that John experienced as he witnessed a New Heaven and a New Earth.

(21) Then I saw "a new heaven and a new earth," for the first heaven and the first earth had passed away, and there was no longer any sea. 2 I saw the Holy City, the New Jerusalem, coming down out of Heaven from God, prepared as a bride beautifully dressed for her husband. 3 And I heard a loud voice from the throne saying, "Look! God's dwelling place is now among the people, and He will dwell with them. They will be His people, and God himself will be with them and be their God. 4 'He will wipe every tear from their eyes. There will be no more death or mourning or crying or pain, for the old order of things has passed away." 5 He who was seated on the throne said, "I am making everything new!" Then He said, "Write this down, for these words are trustworthy and true."

6 He said to me: "It is done." I am the Alpha and the Omega, the Beginning and the End. To the thirsty, I will give water without cost from the spring of the water of life. 7 Those who are victorious will inherit all this, and I will be their God, and they will be my children. 8 But the cowardly, the unbelieving, the vile, the murderers, the sexually immoral, those who practice

magic arts, the idolaters, and all liars—they will be consigned to the fiery lake of burning sulfur; this is the second death."

John sees a new heaven and new earth because the present heaven and earth are gone, and the new earth no longer has any sea; while writing this, the vision of a smaller planet with just land surface a new creation because the sea was no longer of any use. The sea kept people and nations separated and prevented people from uniting readily. With God's presence on earth, the earth was smaller and more comfortable to journey from one end to another. God's dwelling place is now among us. A new Holy City becomes the New Jerusalem. God will provide water of life to drink, and they will be his children.

Earlier in our journey, I mentioned the shortening of the day to 16 hours by increasing the earth's rotation around the earth's axis. The result would be that the earth's diameter would reduce, mountains would fall, and the sea would shrink and even disappear. Here in the chapter, we read that the new world has no sea. Therefore, the landmasses have come together.

The New Jerusalem, the Bride of the Lamb

9 One of the seven angels who had the seven bowls full of the seven last plagues came and said to me, "Come, I will show you the bride, the wife of the Lamb." 10 And he carried me away in the Spirit to a mountain great and high, and showed me the Holy City, Jerusalem, coming down out of heaven from God. 11 It shone with the glory of God, and its brilliance was like that of a very precious jewel, like a

jasper, clear as crystal. 12 It had a great, high wall with twelve gates and with twelve angels at the gates. On the gates were written the names of the twelve tribes of Israel. 13 There were three gates on the East, three on the North, three on the South, and three on the West. 14 The wall of the city had twelve foundations, and on them were the names of the twelve apostles of the Lamb.15 "The angel who talked with me had a measuring rod of gold to measure the city, its gates, and its walls."

16 "The City was laid out like a square, as long as it was wide. He measured the city with the rod and found it to be 12,000 stadia in length and as wide and high as it is long. 17 The angel measured the wall using human measurement, and it was 144 cubits thick. 18 The wall was made of jasper, and the city of pure gold, as pure as glass. 19 The foundations of the city walls were decorated with every kind of precious stone. The first foundation was jasper, the second sapphire, the third agate, the fourth emerald, 20 the fifth onyx, the sixth ruby, the seventh chrysolite, the eighth beryl, the ninth topaz, the tenth turquoise, the eleventh jacinth, and the twelfth amethyst. 21 The twelve gates were twelve pearls, each gate made of a single pearl. The great street of the city was of gold, as pure as transparent glass."

22 "I did not see a temple in the city because the Lord God Almighty and the Lamb are its temples. 23 The City does not need the sun or the moon to shine on it, for the glory of God gives it light, and the Lamb is its lamp. 24 The nations will walk by its light, and the kings of the earth will bring their splendor into it. 25 On no day will its gates ever be shut, for there will be

no night there. 26 The glory and honor of the nations will be brought into it. 27 Nothing impure will ever enter it, nor will anyone who does what is shameful or deceitful, but only those whose names are written in the Lamb's book of life."

Here we have John describing God's new Holy City. I am sure that it is as beautiful if not more so, and I hope that my family, friends, and I may be able to see it in all of its glory. Indeed, there will be no need for a Temple or a Church, and yes, there will not be a Pope or High Priest, for the Lamb of God is both King and High Priest. This is because God has come to dwell with mankind on earth.

Eden Restored

We now watch John for the last time before the curtain closes.

(22) "Then the angel showed me the river of the water of life, as clear as crystal, flowing from the throne of God and of the Lamb 2 down the middle of the great street of the city. On each side of the river stood the tree of life, bearing twelve crops of fruit, yielding its fruit every month. And the leaves of the tree are for the healing of the nations. 3 No longer will there be any curse. The Throne of God and the Lamb will be in the city, and his servants will serve him. 4 They will see his face, and his name will be on their foreheads. 5 There will be no more nights. They will not need the light of a lamp or the light of the sun, for the Lord God will give them light. And they will reign forever and ever."

As I write this, I am tired of all the evil in this world, the lying, cheating, stealing, killing, and hate done not only by individuals but also by the elite leaders of nations for their desire for power. How beautiful and peaceful my spirit would be to see this very image that John saw. How blessed was John to see the Father and the Son on their Thrones in Heaven? Where the light of God's illumination surrounds us and is in our very being. Imagine how beautiful it will be to be standing in the light of God's presence and to feel His Love and Mercy forever. Imagine a place where you have no cares, sorrow, or needs of any kind. I can feel a bit of His light fill me with peace and tranquility as I imagine and write this. What a beautiful feeling it must be! No wonder Moses' face glowed because of being in God's presence. "They saw that his face was radiant. Then Moses would put the veil back over his face until he went in to speak with the Lord." (Exodus 34:35 NIV)

John and the Angel

6 The angel said to me, "These words are trustworthy and true. The Lord, the God who inspires the prophets, sent his angel to show his servants the things that must soon take place."

Here, we read the word 'soon' take place as we have journeyed through the book of Revelation. We have witnessed through the writings and by investigating that some of the events have taken place while others have yet to take place.

7 "Look, I am coming soon! Blessed is the one who keeps the words of the prophecy written in this scroll."

Here, we have a blessing for keeping these words. I, for one, have received much, not in the way of material things. My benefits are in the spirit and knowledge. I can stand fast to the end, not by my human ability but by the grace of the Lord.

8 "I, John, am the one who heard and saw these things. And when I had heard and seen them, I fell down to worship at the feet of the angel who had been showing them to me. 9 But he said to me, 'Don't do that! I am a fellow servant with you and with your

fellow prophets and with all who keep the words of this scroll. Worship God!'"

The angel first refuses to be placed in a position of worship. Second, it presents testimony against the idolatrous worship of saints and angels. Third, it affirms that saints and angels are fellow servants, together in a common bond of devotion and service to the same Lord. Therefore, we praise along with the saints and angels. Together, we are to perform tasks. In the service of the Lord, and call on each other for help to do so.

10 "Then he told me, 'Do not seal up the words of the prophecy of this scroll because the time is near. 11 Let the one who does wrong continue to do wrong; let the vile person continue to be vile; let the one who does right continue to do right, and let the holy person continue to be holy.'"

At first, verse eleven gave me a problem, 'the one who does wrong continues to do wrong,' troubled me. I stopped reading and writing and just let the words filter into my mind. As I prayed for an answer since we share God's Word, "Do not seal up the words" became evident. The meaning doesn't keep the Words hidden but provides everyone with an opportunity to read them. Hence, when the Bible is held open, it will affect men; the filthy, wicked, and unjust will increase in their unrighteousness, but it will also confirm, strengthen, and further sanctify those righteous with God.

Epilogue: Invitation and Warning

12 "Look, I am coming soon! My reward is with me, and I will give to each person according to what they have done. 13 I am the Alpha and the Omega, the First and the Last, the Beginning and the End."

When John heard this, he must have thought that Jesus would be coming before he passed on. Since he would have remembered Christ saying, "Truly I tell you, this generation will certainly not pass away until all these things have happened." (Matt 24:34 NIV). Therefore, the Christians of the First and Second Century thought Christ would soon return. Even Jesus did not know when He was returning. "But about that day or hour, no one knows, not even the angels in heaven, nor the Son, but only the Father." (Matt 24:36 NIV)

There is a straightforward reason why only God knows the hour because you don't let the enemy know when you are coming so that they can prepare. The purpose of this is so Satan does not know when his final hour will occur. What would you do if you knew when you were going to die? Would you party like crazy and sin up to the day you're going to die and ask for forgiveness? Then, God will know your plan. You cannot fool God, so it is better not knowing, thinking today is my last day.

14 "Blessed are those who wash their robes, that they may have the right to the tree of life and may go through the gates into the city. 15 Outside are the dogs, those who practice magic arts, the sexually immoral, the murderers, the idolaters, and everyone who loves and practices falsehood."

Today, news broadcast stations prefer to deceive viewers with fake news, a much kinder phrase than lies. The liberals would have us believe that homosexuality and even pedophilia are normal and excellent behavior.

16 "I, Jesus, have sent my angel to give you this testimony for the churches. I am the Root and the Offspring of David and the bright Morning Star."

17 "The Spirit and the bride say, 'Come!' And let the one who hears say, 'Come!' Let the one who is thirsty come, and let the one who wishes take the free gift of the water of life."

The Lord invites us to come to the spring of flowing water of life. We only need to accept the invitation and live a righteous life of faith in the Lord Jesus Christ.

18 "I warn everyone who hears the words of the prophecy of this scroll: If anyone adds anything to them, God will add to that person the plagues described in this scroll. 19 And if anyone takes words away from this scroll of prophecy, God will take away from that person any share in the tree of life and in the Holy City, which are described in this scroll."

I already touched on this at the very beginning of this writing. However, God does not want to be misquoted about the importance of being very careful in both translation and interpretation.

20 "He who testifies to these things says, 'Yes, I am coming soon.' Amen, Come, Lord Jesus."

I sure wish this final episode, known as Revelation, was all over and done. But Jesus has returned, and God's Throne is on Earth. Praise God, what a glorious day that will be.

21 "The grace of the Lord Jesus be with God's people, Amen!"

A new Eden and the Drama have come full circle. The last scene is in the Garden of Eden, where it all begins with Adam and Eve. The place where evil entered the world, where Babylon once was, is now a new creation. The perfect glory of Eden is once more.

I will conclude this commentary as a well-written essay to close with the problem stated at the beginning of the Bible. "In the beginning, God created the heavens and the earth. 2 Now the earth was formless and empty, darkness was over the surface of the deep, and the Spirit of God was hovering over the waters." (Genesis 1 NIV) The Bible ends with a New Heaven and a New Earth with God's presence to light up the world. God has completed His task of eliminating darkness and all of its evil and replaced it with only His Light.

God's people are those who believe in his Son, Jesus Christ. These are God's people. Those who reject His Son reject Him. Amen, Amen, Praise God! Let us now pray that the Lord God speeds up the timetable, finally brings an end to evil, and creates the New Heaven and Earth that He promised. Amen!

Appendix

Sources

New International Version of the Bible

Babylonian Judaism

http://www.philtar.ac.uk/encyclopedia/judaism/bab-jud.html

Destiny Foundation

http://www.jewishdestiny.com/

SECTION 1 – PART 1

THE ORIGINS & HISTORY OF SEPHARDIC JEWRY

New World encyclopedia

http://www.newworldencyclopedia.org/entry/Phoenician_Civilization

Charles Templeton, Farewell to God, Toronto: McClelland and Stewart, 1999, 71

John Darby, The Origin of Rapture False doctrine: 1830 AD

Lt. Col. Gordon "Jack" Mohr, A.U.S. Ret., The Plot To Destroy Christianity! Honorary Brig. Gen.

Richard Dawkins, The God Delusion, Great Britain: Bantam Press, 2006, 31.

Citizen's Emergency Defense System

https://israelect.com/reference/JackMohr/jm011.htm

About the Author

Anthony "Doc" Raimondo is the founder and President/CEO of Accelerating Evolution LLC, a producer, director, author, keynote speaker, Christian life coach, and teacher. He holds two master's degrees, one in Educational, the other in Communication, and a Doctorate in Educational Supervision. In addition, a doctorate in Theology. These degrees have taught him how to conduct research and live God's will in our lives.

"Doc," as an educator and life coach, teaches that knowledge of a personal theme, God's plan for your life. The purpose of providing Christians with opportunities to share their God-given talent with humanity is to evolve both the performer and the audience to the spiritual development that God inspires us to obtain.

Dr. Raimondo has spent his life from his teen years studying the Scripture and various doctrines. He believes in the most excellent story ever written in the Bible. Raimondo has taught reading and writing for 20 years and thinks many theologians ignore a complete saga's literary position from beginning to end.

"Doc" also has brought his verbal storytelling skills to the printed word in the Least of Brothers Series based on two verses from the Bible, Matthew 25:40 and verse 45. "What you did, or did not do, for the least of brothers or sisters you did or did not do to me." 'Doc' has IMDb credits for a feature film as an associate producer of Silver Twins and producer credit for The Johnson Show. He has also produced an Internet Radio program, Doc Speaks Show on Intention Radio, and over 160 YouTube videos. He has also co-produced several Off-Broadway Theatre Productions written by Antony Raymond, Julio, Pretty Babies, Lustiness, Gin & Milk, and Apt. 301, and Yeah, I Met This Girl. A dance performance of The Savior Project and the Gitrite Comedy Show at a cafe theatre in Newark, NJ.

For more information:

https://www.anthonyfraimondo.com
https://www.youtube.com/c/drraimondo
or write "Doc" at: doc@anthonyfraimondo.com

Made in the USA
Middletown, DE
10 May 2024